Naked Forex

Founded in 1807, John Wiley & Sons is the oldest independent publishing company in the United States. With offices in North America, Europe, Australia and Asia, Wiley is globally committed to developing and marketing print and electronic products and services for our customers' professional and personal knowledge and understanding.

The Wiley Trading series features books by traders who have survived the market's ever changing temperament and have prospered—some by reinventing systems, others by getting back to basics. Whether a novice trader, professional or somewhere in-between, these books will provide the advice and strategies needed to prosper today and well into the future.

For a list of available titles, please visit our Web site at www.WileyFinance.com.

Naked Forex

High-Probability Techniques for Trading without Indicators

ALEX NEKRITIN
WALTER PETERS, PhD

WILEY

John Wiley & Sons, Inc.

Published by John Wiley & Sons, Inc., Hoboken, New Jersey.
Published simultaneously in Canada.

For general information on our other products and services or for technical support, please contact our Customer Care Department within the United States at (800) 762-2974, outside the United States at (317) 572-3993 or fax (317) 572-4002.

Wiley also publishes its books in a variety of electronic formats. Some content that appears in print may not be available in electronic books. For more information about Wiley products, visit our web site at www.wiley.com.

Library of Congress Cataloging-in-Publication Data:

Nekritin, Alex, 1980-
  Naked Forex : high-probability techniques for trading without indicators / Alex Nekritin, Walter Peters.
    p. cm. – (Wiley trading ; 534)
  Includes index.
  ISBN 978-1-118-11401-8 (cloth); ISBN 978-1-118-22435-9 (ebk);
  ISBN 978-1-118-26244-3 (ebk); ISBN 978-1-118-23749-6 (ebk)
  1. Foreign exchange market. 2. Foreign exchange futures. 3. Speculation.
I. Peters, Walter, 1973- II. Title.
  HG3821.N45 2012
  332.4'5–dc23

                                                            2011043306

Printed in the United States of America

SKY10076255_060124

For all gun traders as well as those rude and cute possums of the world.

Contents

Foreword

The Internet engendered the online trading phenomenon. One can trade anywhere there is a connection to the World Wide Web. The result has also been the creation of instant experts, trading gurus who offer modern versions of snake-oil cures for traders. The web is flooded with trading alerts, systems, and blogs that promise returns that will lead to instant wealth. Most of the books in the field fail to provide actionable knowledge. In this environment, Alex Nekritin and Walter Peters in *Naked Forex: High-Probability Techniques for Trading without Indicators* provide an honest and effective presentation about forex trading that certainly beginners need, and that more experienced traders forget they need.

Naked Forex makes some powerful points about trading forex that really apply to other markets as well. First and foremost, price is the most important indicator of all. All indicators are derived from price. Many traders have forgotten this fact because computerization has made it easy to generate new indicators. Indicators work more like training wheels for learning to ride a bicycle. They are temporary in their capacity to help traders build their skills. They actually limit the evolution of a trader's performance because they provide a disincentive to "listen" to the market. *Naked Forex* goes into detail on how a trading signal that is indicator-based is inferior to what Nekritin and Peters call a "naked" signal.

Another key insight that the book provides is the importance of knowing one's personality in trading. Trading systems that are based on untested algorithms that are purely technical will surely fail. Nekritin and Peters argue that trading systems should reflect decisions that traders would make that are based on looking at charts. Manual backtesting, they suggest, is an effective way to identify a trading system's strengths and weaknesses.

A third major focus of *Naked Forex* is the concept of identifying support and resistance zones. The fact is that with the trillions of dollars that float each hour through the currency markets, prices reach certain levels and stop. One can try to figure out why they stop rising or stop falling. But the job of the trader is to observe accurately where the price is and where it came from. Price zones provide the naked truth about market sentiment. If a price breaks through a zone, no matter what the reason, it is a signal—and a more powerful signal than any indicator. Nekritin and Peters call these points of price action market scars. It is a good metaphor because markets have memory and so do traders. The authors introduce the "last-kiss trade" as a powerful tool in identifying when breakouts have occurred. The book is filled with gems that provide visualizations of price action, such as the big shadow, kangaroo tails, and the big belt.

As someone who has been training people on how to trade forex for nearly 13 years, I welcome this book as one that stands out as a basic manual on how to evaluate and trade the increasingly chaotic forex markets. I will use it for my students.

Abe Cofnas
author of *Trading Binary Options* (Bloomberg) and
editor of *The Fear and Greed Trader Newsletter*,
Agora Financial, Inc.

Preface

U nfortunately, most forex traders lose out. Profitable trading is reserved for the select few. Expectations drive reality for many things in life, and successful trading is no different. Most forex traders have three preconceptions about successful trading. These are the three myths of successful trading, and the structure of this book is based on each of these myths.

Myth 1: Successful trading must be indicator based. The first part of this book dispels this myth. There are many ways to profit in forex, some of them do involve indicators, but indicators are not necessary for successful trading. There are professional traders around the globe, many of them good friends of mine, who use "naked" charts to make trading decisions. In some ways, indicators delay the progression of the trader because the focus is on the indicator, rather than price action. Indicators become the scapegoat for losing streaks and often keep losing traders in a holding pattern. It is much easier for the novice trader to begin trading without indicators from the beginning.

Myth 2: Successful trading must be complex. The second part of this book is about naked trading systems. These systems are incredibly simple. Do not confuse simplicity with ineptitude. Although these systems are simple when applied correctly, they may also yield big profits and build confidence in your trading. You may view this as the meat of the book, the most important section, but I disagree. I think the third section is the most critical to your trading success.

Myth 3: Successful trading is dependent on the trading system. This is probably the most widely held belief among traders. This is precisely why there are thousands of trading systems on the market, all promising great riches to the brave traders who pony up the money for the next Holy Grail. Many veteran traders understand the importance of trading psychology. Personal beliefs and attitudes toward risk are the greatest predictors of trading success, and the trading system is not nearly as important as many traders assume. For most traders, after years of trading, this fact becomes apparent. The third section of the book concerns trading psychology and how you may both identify and change your thinking, because this is the real driving factor in your trading success.

Many readers will continue to hold onto these myths. In fact, some readers (those who believe trading success depends on the trading system) will simply read the second section and begin trading the naked trading systems. This is unfortunate. The first section is critical because it offers reasons for price action trading (a new belief system) and a course of action for becoming an expert at naked trading (new trading habits). The third section is where breakeven and slightly profitable traders will learn to move into the realm of the true professional trader. All sections of the book are important, and it is my hope that by reading it you will find simple methods for extracting profits from the market.

You can trade successfully without indicators. For many traders, naked trading is both refreshing and easy to apply. You can trade successfully with simple trading systems. Simple systems are robust and powerful. However, ultimately, your success as a trader will depend, not on the trading system, but on how you incorporate your beliefs and attitudes about risk into your trading routine. I hope this book will aid you in your journey to trading success.

I also hope that you keep in touch by stopping by the companion web site for this book, complete with live market trades, additional tools, and new naked trading systems. You will find this on the Web at www.fxjake.com/book.

Walter Peters, PhD
Sydney, Australia
October 2011

Acknowledgments

There are many people who deserve acknowledgment for this book. The list includes but is not limited to the following: Meg Freeborn for patience and unique ability to turn rough stones into polished gems (I know because I have seen her do it). Eddie Kwong deserves credit for putting this book idea in front of the right people. Sean Lydiard is living proof that six degrees of separation is fact. Arshia Bolour, who is a true brother in every sense of the word. Abe Cofnas, for his patience and kindness in helping me with the conversion from trader to trading author. Evan Burton for believing in the book idea and making it happen. Colin Jessup for his unique perspective on naked trading. My brother Ashkan Bolour, who introduced me to the world of forex so many years ago. My parents for unconditionally supporting me in every endeavor. My dissertation committee (and Dr. David Estes in particular) who taught me years ago how to write so that others could understand me. My sister for always being there for me. And to the first-line editor Melissa McConaghy—without your help, I am certain this book would not have happened.

—W.P.

PART ONE

Naked Forex Trading Revealed

CHAPTER 1

The Fundamentals of Forex Trading

Gregory: *"Draw thy tool ..."*
Sampson: *"My naked weapon is out."*
—Shakespeare, *Romeo and Juliet*

Welcome to the world of forex trading. Forex is the largest market in the world. Forex traders exchange $4 trillion each day, but is forex the best market for you? The answer depends on what you are looking for. If you want a market that never sleeps, if you want the opportunity to trade at any time of the day, if you would like to make a boatload of money in a short amount of time, forex may be for you (it should be noted that you may also lose an incredible amount of money in a short amount of time). Traders with very little money can begin trading forex. In forex, you may take relatively large trades with small amounts of money because of the favorable leverage requirements. There are many reasons to become a forex trader, but before jumping into the reasons, perhaps we should take a closer look at the characteristics of a forex trade.

A QUICK LESSON IN CURRENCIES

"Forex" is simply an abbreviation for "foreign exchange." All foreign exchange transactions involve two currencies. If an individual trader, a bank, a government, a corporation, or a tourist in a Hawaiian print shirt on a tropical island decides to exchange one currency for another, a forex trade takes place. In every instance, one currency is being bought and, simultaneously, another currency is being sold. Currencies must be compared to something else in order to establish value; this is why forex trading involves two currencies.

If you and I go to the beach and I tell you the tide is low right now, how do you know this is true? You may decide to compare the current water level to the pier. If there are starfish and mussels exposed on the pier, you may believe me because you can compare the current water level to the previous water level. In forex, we compare currencies in much the same way, currencies are traded in pairs and, thus, one currency is always compared to another currency.

An example may be helpful to illustrate how currencies are traded. If you are a hotshot forex trader, and you believe that the EUR/USD is going to go up, you may decide to buy the EUR/USD. Thus, you think that the Euro currency will get stronger, and the U.S. dollar will weaken. You are buying the EUR/USD currency pair, another way to look at this is to say you are buying Euros and simultaneously selling U.S. dollars. The unique (and often difficult to understand) aspect of forex trading to keep in mind is this: Each forex transaction involves the buying of one currency pair and simultaneously the selling of another currency pair.

If you have experience buying or selling in any market—the stock market, a futures market, an options market, the baseball card market, or the used car market—then you understand markets. For any market transaction a buyer wants to buy something and a seller wants to get rid of something. The forex market is simply a money market, the place where speculators exchange one currency for another. In many ways, the forex market is no different from the stock market. The major differences between forex and the stock market are as follows: A forex transaction involves buying one currency pair and selling another, also, the symbols to identify forex pairs are consistent and systematic, unlike the symbols used to identify companies listed on a stock exchange.

Forex traders buy and sell countries. It is true: Forex traders are basically buying "shares" in a country, just as a stock trader buys shares in a company. For example, if forex trader Emma decides to sell the EUR/USD, she is essentially selling the European Union (and buying the United States). To be even more specific, we might suggest Emma is buying the *economy* of the United States, and selling the *economy* of the European Union. Does this mean that Emma must keep tabs on all the economic data for all the countries that she is trading? The short answer is no, but we will talk more about news and trading based on economic news and data a bit further on in this book.

Just as a stock has a symbol, so do currencies. Table 1.1 illustrates the most popular currencies and their symbols. Do you notice a pattern? There is a secret code for currencies. The three-letter code for each currency pair is composed of the country (first two letters) and the name of the currency

TABLE 1.1 Major Currencies of the World

Country	Currency	Symbol	Nickname
Euro Zone	Euro	EUR	Fiber
United States	Dollar	USD	Greenback
Japan	Yen	JPY	Yen
Great Britain	Pound	GBP	Cable
Switzerland	Franc	CHF	Swissy
Australia	Dollar	AUD	Aussie
New Zealand	Dollar	NZD	Kiwi

(last letter). So, for example, the Japanese yen is JPY, the "JP" stands for Japan, and the "Y" stands for Yen. The currencies listed in Table 1.1 are the major currencies; these are the most widely traded currencies.

PLAYERS OF THE FOREX MARKET

The forex market is an enormous, growing market. Forex trading doubled from 2004 to 2010, and today the amount of money traded in forex each day is staggering. The New York Stock Exchange, the world's largest stock market, turns over about $75 billion each day. Forex traders trade *five times* that amount each day.

You often hear people claim that because the forex market is so large, it is relatively easy for forex traders to jump in and ride the trends in this gigantic market, the world's largest market. However, most forex traders trade what is called the retail forex market; this is a different market (akin to a parallel universe) to the "real" forex market in which $4 trillion is exchanged each day. In essence, there are two markets in forex. There is the interbank market, where banks, hedge funds, governments, and corporations exchange currencies, and there is the retail market. Most forex traders trade in the retail forex market, an entirely different market to the "real" interbank market.

In the retail forex market, your competition is the other forex traders trading the retail forex market, and, believe it or not, your broker. When you make money trading forex, these other traders in the retail market lose, and so does your broker. Most retail forex traders do not make money. In fact, your forex broker will assume that you are going to lose money in the long run. This is a perfectly reasonable assumption, since the large majority of forex traders lose money.

Would you like to know about the secret that forex brokers don't want you to know? Here it is: Forex brokers divide all traders into two groups. There are the winners—these are the forex traders who make money—and then there are the losers—these are the forex traders who lose money. Guess which group all new forex traders get put into? Retail forex brokers believe that all new customers are unlikely to make money, so all new accounts are placed into the loser group. After several months of consistently profitable Forex trading a trader may be placed into the winner group.

It may sound surprising, but it is true. If you start making money trading forex over several months, you will join the winners. Your retail forex broker will begin to hedge your trades. In other words, if you are in the winner group, your retail forex broker will take trades in the real forex market, the interbank market, to offset the profits accumulated by the winner group. For example, if most of the traders in the winner group have decided to buy the EUR/USD, then the broker will put in a trade to buy the EUR/USD in the interbank market in the hopes that, if the winners are correct, the forex broker can use the profits in the interbank market to pay the winning traders. This is how your retail forex broker deals with winning traders.

What about losing traders? Since most forex traders are losing traders, your forex broker assumes that you will not make money when you open up an account. Only after you have consistently made money trading forex will your broker become concerned with your trading. Guess what happens to all of those losing trades? Those losing trades fatten your broker's pocket. All losing trades are "business profits" for your broker. This is because your broker takes the other side of your forex trade. Although it is true that some retail forex brokers match up trade orders so that a trader with a buy trade order is paired up with a trader with a sell trade. However, the overwhelming majority of retail forex brokers do not do this. Unless you are a consistently winning trader, your broker will take the risk on your trades, and assume that your trades will lose money in the long run. This is not something that is widely discussed, but it is true. Your forex broker wants you to lose, because your losses are your broker's profits.

How would you like to make the jump from the group of losing traders to the group of winning traders? Would you like to join the 5 percent of winning traders? I know you can join the 5 percent, and I will show you precisely how you can leap into the group of winners in later chapters.

TOOLS OF THE TRADE: FUNDAMENTAL VERSUS TECHNICAL INDICATORS

So, how do forex traders decide when to buy or sell? There are basically two schools of traders, and you must decide which school fits your trading personality. The first school is the school of fundamental analysis. Fundamental traders use economic reports and news reports as the basis for their trading decisions. Forex traders who have a fundamental approach will closely examine world events, interest-rate decisions, and political news. Fundamental traders are concerned with properly interpreting news, whereas the focus for the technical forex trader is quite different.

The technical forex trader uses technical indicators (or "indicators") to properly interpret price movement on a chart. The forex trader who adopts a technical, indicator-based approach will examine the price charts. So, while the fundamental forex trader is concerned with interpreting news and world events, the technical trader is concerned with interpreting price on a chart.

What are technical indicators? Indicators are simply another way of looking at a market price. In much the same way that it is possible to examine the speed of a car in many different ways, it is possible to examine price charts in many different ways, with indicators. Just for a moment, consider how many different ways you may measure the speed of a car:

- Measured in kilometers per hour.
- Measured in miles per hour.
- Measured in the time it takes to travel one mile.
- Measured by the time it takes to accelerate to 60 mph.
- Measured by how quickly the car can stop.

Likewise, there are many ways to look at price on a chart. There are more technical indicators than telephone call centers in India.

WHAT IS NAKED FOREX?

It can be very confusing for the novice trader, and this is one reason why naked trading, trading without indicators, can be liberating. When starting out, many traders focus on the indicator. This is completely understandable since nearly 90 percent of the forex trading books, the vast majority of forex sites on the Internet, and forex trading seminars focus on indicators and indicator-based trading.

Indicators encourage "secondary thinking," which is a real handicap for traders looking to acquire expertise. Secondary thinking involves analyzing the *indicator*, spending time considering where the *indicator* may go, rather than focusing on the market. Naked traders, by definition, focus on the market, which is very different.

Focusing on indicators may be one of the primary reasons that some forex traders do not make money. Indicators can be confusing, unhelpful, and just plain wrong. In the next chapter we take a look at technical trading, and some of the tragic trading mistakes forex traders make, and how to avoid them by adopting the naked-trading approach.

CHAPTER 2

Avoiding a Trading Tragedy

Out of intense complexities intense simplicities emerge.

—Winston Churchill

I f you are reading this book, you are probably a technical trader. You may have spent time, money, and effort learning about indicators. You may have learned through experience that trading with indicators can be very difficult. In some ways, trading with indicators makes it difficult to find profits. Perhaps a close look at *why* indicator-based trading systems have difficulty finding profits in forex is in order.

All indicators are created from price data. This is what *all* indicators do to price data: Price data enters into an equation and is spit out as something else. Sometimes the end product is a squiggly line, sometimes a straight line, sometimes a color or a number; it depends on the indicator. The end result is always the same: The indicator changes *price data via a formula*. The form of this end result (the indicator) may vary, but the process is always the same.

These very same indicators, based on price data, are meant to hint at future movements in the market. Stated another way, an indicator will suck in price data, massage and process these data, and then spit out a graphical representation of these data. Indicators offer price data in another form. Perhaps this new form of price data is easier to interpret; perhaps this new form of the price data will hint at what the market may do in the near future. All indicator-based trading systems are founded on the idea that price data is in a better form when presented as an indicator. Trade decisions

9

based on indicators *assume* that the data in indicator form is more valuable than raw price data.

INDICATOR

A metric derived from price data. Historical price data—such as the open, close, high, and low—are entered into a formula to calculate the metric. This metric is then represented graphically to anticipate and interpret market movements.

Traders want to know where price will go in the future. Traders pay millions upon millions of dollars for educational seminars, DVDs, website lessons and, yes, even books such as this one. The great hope for most traders is that there is a valuable indicator (or recipe of indicators) that will hint at where the market is headed in the future. Millions upon millions of dollars are spent each year by traders (and also investment companies, hedge funds, banks, etc.) because a slight edge may provide millions of dollars in profits. In forex a slight edge may mean billions of dollars in profits.

IS THERE A "BETTER" INDICATOR?

Which indicator is best? Which suite of indicators offers a clear edge in the markets? Perhaps it is best to find out who is making money in forex, and then do what they do. Which is the magic formula? Unfortunately, the answer to this question is "It depends on who you ask." This may very well be the correct answer. As we will see later in the book, trading is often relative and rarely, if ever, a one-size-fits-all endeavor. Some indicators are considered shams, others are misinterpreted by the masses, and still others are best used *contrary to their original design intent*. Indicators may be incorrect. What if the indicator is correct, but a bit slow to hint at the direction the market will take? The indicator *might* provide valuable information, but might also be slow to the party, and thus not of much value. Perhaps a slight *change* to the indicator formula will speed it up a bit.

Perhaps indicators are similar to a wristwatch, constantly improving, more features available as needed, but would it be possible to take a wristwatch, and manipulate time by running a formula through the hours, the minutes, and the seconds displayed on the wristwatch? Would the wristwatch keep better time once the formula manipulated the *actual time* of the day?

Using a formula to create a better time on a wristwatch may seem weird and counterproductive, but this is precisely what indicators *may* accomplish by changing and massaging price data. Indicator-based trading is taking a wristwatch and changing the time with a complex formula in the hopes that the wristwatch will somehow tell time better. Who wants a wristwatch with something other than the real time displayed? Do indicators (all of which are calculated using price data) allow us to understand price better?

Perhaps it is best to put aside any philosophical differences with technical indicators. Let us assume that our indicator is based upon a magical formula and this formula allows us to get a glimpse of the future. Our indicator magically transforms price data into some other number, color, or line, and suggests where price is headed in the near future. Unfortunately, *even if* our indicator is able to accomplish this, difficulties may endure with indicator-based trading.

Indicators are inherently slow. The market will be moving up long before an indicator suggests it is time to buy. Likewise, an indicator will suggest it is time to sell long after the market has started falling. This is one of the main complaints with indicators: they lag behind price. This is a fair concern. Figure 2.1 contains an AUD/USD four-hour chart with the Relative Strength Index (RSI) indicator. Traditionally, there are two RSI signals. If the RSI is above the 70 level, the market is overbought, and once the RSI falls back down below 70, a sell trade is initiated.

Likewise, if the RSI falls below 30, the market is said to be oversold, and, traditionally, a buy trade is signaled once the RSI moves back above 30 (see arrow in Figure 2.2).

In these examples we see that the RSI indicator suggests a trade at *about* the right time. The market turned around near the RSI signal in both examples. However, the RSI did not signal a trade at the precise turning point in the market. To find these turning points, an indicator of a different type is required. One of the primary reasons why naked trading is so attractive to forex traders is because naked trading allows for *early entries into trades*. Indicators may alert traders to the fact that the market has turned around *after the market has turned around*, but naked traders may find turning points in the market *as they occur*. Naked trading strategies are based on the current price of the market, and, therefore, they allow for an earlier entry. Indicator-based trade signals will lag because it takes time for the price data to be processed through the formulas that make up the indicator.

INDICATOR LAG

Significant moves in the forex market occur before a technical indicator provides a signal.

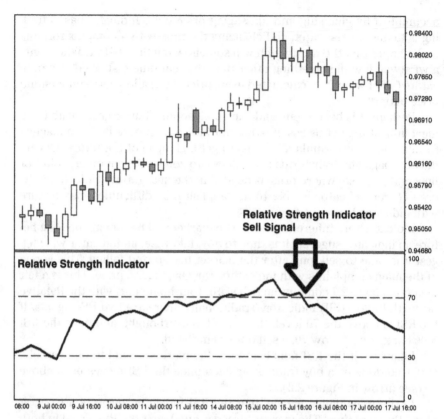

FIGURE 2.1 Traditional RSI Sell Signal on AUD/USD 4-Hour Chart.
© 2000–2011, MetaQuotes Software Corp.

Naked traders have an incredible advantage. Entering a trade early often means the entry price is closer to the stop loss price. A tighter stop loss may mean more profits, the precise reason for this is examined later in the book. After mastering a few simple strategies, naked traders find it very difficult to move back to indicator-based strategies simply because naked-trading strategies remove the lag time that is inherent with indicator-based trading.

Here is another example, this time with the EUR/USD daily chart (Figure 2.3). In this example the indicator at the bottom of the chart is the Moving Average Convergence Divergence (MACD). The construction and theory behind the MACD is not important, the MACD consists of a few moving averages. The critical signal for the MACD is when the two moving averages cross (see the dark circle in Figure 2.3). A traditional buy signal

FIGURE 2.2 Traditional RSI Buy Signal on AUD/USD 4-Hour Chart.
© 2000–2011, MetaQuotes Software Corp.

occurs when the MACD has been traveling lower for some time and then turns around, and the faster-moving average crosses the slower-moving average.

In Figure 2.3 the EUR/USD daily chart has been falling for some time. Price starts to turn around and trade higher, and consequently the MACD moving averages start to creep upward. Finally, we see the faster-moving average on the MACD has crossed above the slower-moving average. This signals a buy trade for the MACD trader. After crossing upward on the MACD, the market does indeed move higher (see Figure 2.4).

Although this trade looks like a nice trade, the naked trader would have entered this trade earlier than the trader using the traditional MACD trading strategy. The naked trader and the MACD trader both profit, but the naked trader is able to enter the trade sooner and use a tighter stop loss.

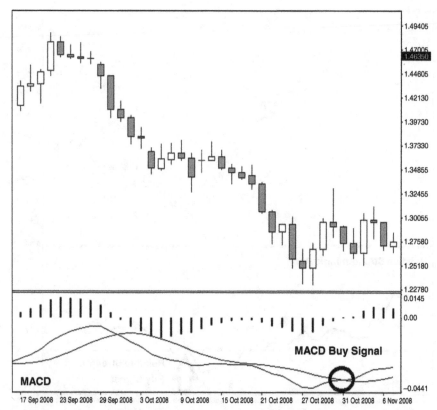

FIGURE 2.3 Traditional MACD Buy Signal on EUR/USD Daily Chart marked with a circle.
© 2000–2011, MetaQuotes Software Corp.

Tighter stops mean more money. The naked trader and the MACD trader could have both exited at the same price, but the naked trader captures more profits because the stop loss is placed closer to the entry price. The money-management section of this book will have more information on how naked trading strategies enable traders to make more money simply because naked signals appear earlier than indicator-based trading signals.

The MACD and the RSI are not the only indicators that lag. All indicators lag. The stochastic is a popular indicator used to time trades according to the natural rhythms of the market. One traditional stochastic trading method is similar to the RSI strategy. A sell signal is indicated when the stochastic falls below the 30 level and then crosses higher (see Figure 2.5).

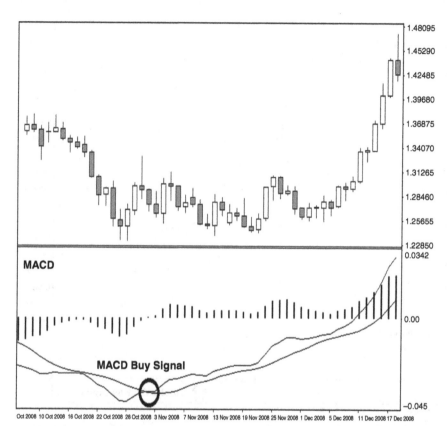

FIGURE 2.4 The EUR/USD trades higher after the traditional MACD Buy Signal on EUR/USD Daily Chart.
© 2000–2011, MetaQuotes Software Corp.

PIPS

A "pip" is a percentage in point. One pip is equal to 1/100th of 1 percent. It has traditionally marked the smallest move a forex pair can make. Forex traders track trades in terms of pips. However, many brokers are now using "pipettes"—these are 1/1000th of 1 percent units.

The EUR/USD 1-hour chart shows the stochastic falling below 30 on the stochastic. A few hours later, the stochastic crosses upward and rises above 30, a clear buy signal. The stochastic is moving up, so price should follow. However, the market then falls a further *90 pips*. For most traders

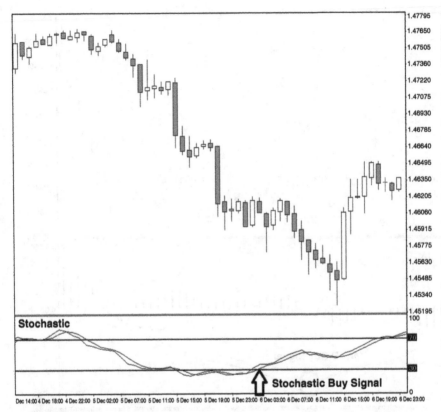

FIGURE 2.5 EUR/USD 1-Hour Chart—Traditional Buy Signal on the Oversold Stochastic.
© 2000–2011, MetaQuotes Software Corp.

this trade would be a big loser. What about the naked trader? In this instance, the naked trader gets a very clear buy signal after the stochastic buy signal (see Figure 2.6).

What happens after the naked trading signal? The market jumps more than 40 pips immediately. The naked trader avoids many losing trades by waiting for a *price action signal* and quickly finds profits. Not all naked trades are winners, of course, but this trade is an example of how the naked trader is able to avoid some of the very common indicator-based mistakes because the naked trader uses the price action of the market to determine entry signals.

Notice how the naked trader avoids the drawdown with this trade signal. The market immediately moves in the expected direction, upward, after the signal. Contrast this entry to the stochastic entry signal. The

FIGURE 2.6 EUR/USD 1-Hour Chart—Naked Buy Signal versus Stochastic Buy Signal. The traditional stochastic buy signal occurs immediately before the market falls. The naked trader has a buy signal at the market turning point.
© 2000–2011, MetaQuotes Software Corp.

characteristic indicator lag associated with the stochastic means that the stochastic trader not only enters a losing trade, but immediately after the stochastic signal the market trades in the wrong direction, and the trade enters into a protracted drawdown. In fact, it is unlikely that the stochastic trader ever had profit on this trade. Naked-trading strategies enable the trader to enter a trade based on *current market price action,* and often avoid the severe drawdowns associated with indicator-based trading.

Most traders believe severe drawdowns are a part of trading. This is simply not true. Severe drawdowns are characteristic of *mistimed entry signals,* and most traders use indicators to find entry signals, so most traders mistime entries.

TAKING RESPONSIBILITY FOR LOSING TRADES

All traders experience drawdowns. All traders experience losing trades. However, naked traders take responsibility for losing trades. Indicator-based traders often blame their indicators for unsuccessful trades (e.g., "the MACD *looked* like it was going to cross here," "my indicator did not load correctly," "maybe I should change the settings on my indicator because the market has been choppy lately," "that moving average crossover was a fake out—whipsawed on that one," etc.), but the naked trader does not have this excuse. There is no scapegoat when you are using market data (price action) to take trades. Trading with price action, that is, the actual price on the chart as the basis for all trading decisions, means that the naked trader has no excuse for losing trades. This is extremely liberating for many traders.

The indicator-based trader also has the added advantage of an indicator to blame when things go awry; the naked trader can blame no one but the market for losing trades. This is a subtle but very important difference point of reference for the naked trader. All trading involves an aspect of luck. All traders experience a lucky streak of winning trades and an unlucky streak of losing trades. Without the crutch of indicators, naked traders are more likely to take responsibility for their trading results.

Perhaps we should take a close look at this idea of trading responsibility. If you decide to trade a new trading system, you may have put the system through a screening process. After spending time testing the system, you have convinced yourself that the trading system is worthwhile and will indeed make money over the long run (at this stage your research may far exceed the effort that 90 percent of forex traders put into their trading research). If, after all of your research, when you start trading live you see the first seven trades turn out to be losing trades, you may be discouraged. What would you do? Perhaps you decide to maintain trading the system, and you suffer through an additional three more losing trades. After 10 consecutive losing trades what would you do? Would you stop trading the system? Would you create a new rule to filter out some of losing trades that you have experienced? Would you decide the trading system is no longer profitable, and give up on trading the system? There are many possible explanations for the reason why the trading system failed after you launched it into live action. Maybe the market has changed. Maybe the system no longer works. Perhaps the 10 losing trades were just an unlucky streak.

Your decision, after faced with the 10 losing trades, will place you into one of two groups: the terrible-system group or the bad-market group (only naked traders can avoid these groups). If you are unsure about your group, pay attention to what you think about the next time you have a string of losing trades, you will quickly learn which group is yours.

Terrible-system traders, after a string of 10 losing trades, blame the trading system. Terrible-system traders will say "the trading system is not working anymore" or "this trading system must be modified to get it back on track." Terrible-system traders decide to modify or give up on the trading system after a losing streak. Often, terrible-system traders will suggest adding another indicator or otherwise slightly modifing the trading system to help filter out some of the losing trades recently triggered. The other strategy employed by these traders is to give up on the trading system. "The system is broken," they say, or "This trading system worked well before, but now it is breaking down, all systems have a shelf life, and this trading system has expired," or "the system may have made good profits in the past, but it simply doesn't work anymore."

If you find yourself saying something similar, you are probably a terrible-system trader. If you are constantly changing trading systems, particularly after a losing streak, you are a terrible-system trader. All terrible-system traders blame the *system* when finding profits becomes difficult.

Bad-market traders take a different approach. Bad-market traders analyze the losing trades after a drawdown and instead conclude that the market has changed. Bad-market traders can come up with many reasons that this market is structurally very different from before, and may be heard muttering things like "the Bank of Japan's intervention has changed the market," or "things have changed with the Euro since Spain went bankrupt." The precise reasons may vary, but the essence of the argument remains the same. Sometimes the bad-market trader will use subtle arguments such "the market is too volatile," "there is not enough volume today," "my broker is unable to execute my trades fast enough." The latter argument hints at a common scapegoat for the bad-market trader—the broker.

Bad-market traders are often identified by their willingness to engage in broker conspiracy theories. The fact is that dishonest brokers are found out, and forex traders will eventually abandon the dishonest brokers. Word spreads quickly, particularly among intelligent, Internet-savvy traders with high-speed Internet connections. But for the bad-market trader, the broker offers the perfect excuse for a failing trading system. Bad-market traders place blame on the broker or the market, and thus have a reason for abandoning a losing trading system.

Many bad-market traders engage in fundamental analysis, but not all fundamental traders belong to the bad-market camp. The interpretation of economic data and engaging in fundamental analysis is often an opportunity for bad-market traders to further their argument. These traders will decide to give up on a trading system after a series of losing trades, just as the terrible-system traders decide to abandon a losing system; it is only the *reason* for giving up on the system that varies. The terrible-system trader places blame on the system, and the bad-market trader is convinced the market has fundamentally changed. Both bad-market traders and terrible-system traders will end up searching for an entirely different trading system.

Interestingly, the difference between a terrible-system trader and a bad-market trader is often conscientiousness. The conscientious trader is usually the bad-market trader. This is because the conscientious trader will spend time testing and ensuring that any trading system employed is viable before risking money in the market. The end result of the system testing is confidence in the system for the bad-market trader. For the bad-market trader, the experience of a drawdown is quite harrowing and unexpected, because the trading system has been tested and seems viable; if the system cannot be wrong, the market must be "wrong."

Our terrible-system trader is unlikely to have spent the same effort testing the trading system. The terrible-system trader probably found the system on a forex Internet forum, purchased it from an Internet marketer, learned it from a friend, or perhaps heard a circle of forex traders discussing the system in hushed tones at a party. The terrible-system trader may be trading a profitable system, but without spending the time testing the system, the terrible-system trader is unlikely to hold the system in high regard.

So how might you avoid falling into the terrible system or bad-market groups? What might you do to change your fate? You may want to carefully consider adopting naked trading. Trading naked means trading without indicators, and removing indicators from your chart will make it difficult to adopt the attitude of the terrible-system trader. Also, if you decide to trade naked you will be trading on price action or the market movements. You could blame the market for a string of losing trades as a naked trader, but that would be a bit like blaming the river for being wet.

Naked traders find trades based on market movements, so, unless the market is moving "incorrectly," there is no such thing as a bad market for the naked trader. Naked traders may only blame losing trades on poor execution (the trader's fault) or poor luck (sometimes you flip a coin seven times and it lands on tails every time). Naked traders may find that trading without indicators is extremely liberating.

Traders around the world have found that adopting naked-trading strategies means letting go of a trade. There are no indicators to give false signals, there are no settings to tweak; there is simply the market price and the trading decision. Naked traders have a true advantage because the focus of the trade is the *current market price*. There is no better indicator of the sentiment, attitude, or exuberance of the market than the current market price. Naked traders make the current market price their indicator.

In fact, for many naked traders, the current market price is a bit like a biofeedback machine. I certainly look at the market price as biofeedback. A biofeedback machine will allow you to tune into the physiological changes in your body, in the hopes that you can better control your physiology. For example, if I am an anxious person, and I am always suffering from stress, I can hook myself up to a biofeedback machine. The machine will alert me if I become anxious (blood pressure increases, heart rate increases, etc. would cause the machine to produce the sound) by sounding off an alert. I can then pay attention to the sounds of the machine and use relaxation techniques to decrease my anxiety. The machine simply alerts me when I need to recalibrate my physiology. Over time, I should be able to wean myself off of the biofeedback machine and reduce my anxiety on my own, without the aid of the biofeedback alerts.

LEARNING FROM MARKET BIOFEEDBACK™

It may seem strange, but you will eventually be able to do the same thing with your trades if you decide to adopt naked-trading strategies. In the beginning, the market price is your biofeedback machine. If the market is going in the wrong direction, you have *valuable* feedback on your trade. Learn from this. Was the entry too early? (Most traders I know are much more likely to jump into a trade too early than to wait too late.) Was the entry too late? The market will tell you how your trade rates. Why is it important to pay attention to the market biofeedback? Because you will learn more from Market Biofeedback than you will learn from any guru, any trading book, or any online course. Another way to state this is as follows: Paying close attention to how the market behaves after you enter a trade is one of the best learning tools available to you.

MARKET BIOFEEDBACK

A psychological, behavioral, and trading response to the market price *after* a trade has been entered.

Market Biofeedback involves two distinct domains, The first is how the market reacts (price action) after you enter your trade, and the second is how you react to the price action in the market after you enter your trade. Both parts of the Market Biofeedback equation are needed for you to get a clear picture of what you are learning, and more importantly, what you *should learn*, from your trading experiences. You should learn from the price action the market offers after you enter a trade. You should also learn from your reaction to the market after you enter a trade. Even if you do not consciously intend to learn from Market Biofeedback, it is important for you to recognize that Market Biofeedback will yield all your important trading decisions. How you approach your trading, which trading systems you employ, whether you give up on your trading or go on to a long and successful trading career, *all* these things are determined by Market Biofeedback.

Most traders allow Market Biofeedback to completely dictate their trading approach, *even without realizing* this is happening. For example, some traders start out trading the five-minute charts and then slowly gravitate toward longer timeframes, such as the four-hour or daily charts. Why do these traders do this? The answer is Market Biofeedback. Other traders, after several losing trades, will give up on a trading system and search for a new one. This change in trading strategy is, once again, due to Market Biofeedback. Other traders may trade the exact same trading system and will experience seven losing trades in succession and hold steady, knowing that the current drawdown is simply an aberration. Market Biofeedback is the difference between the traders who give up on a trading system and look for a new strategy and those traders who maintain confidence despite the losing streak.

How you react and respond to a drawdown, to a windfall of pips, or something in between is exceptionally valuable information. The easiest way to see Market Biofeedback is to *record your thoughts as you trade*. You can record your voice before, during, and after a trade. You can take screenshots of the trade before, during, and after. You may also record video of the trade before, during, and after with a desktop-computer recording software.

Here are the important questions to answer as you record Market Biofeedback:

- Where has the market moved since I entered my trade?
- If I looked at the market now, would I take the same trade?
- How do I feel about my trade?
- What do I like about this trade now?
- What do I dislike about this trade now?
- On a scale of 1 (poor decision) to 10 (great decision), where would I rank this trade now?
- If I were not in a trade now, would I take the opposite trade?

If you ask yourself these questions and record your answers before, during, and after the trade, you will have built up a database of your personal Market Biofeedback—an invaluable tool. More importantly, you will bring into conscious awareness how you react to the market. Most traders will trade their whole lives without recognizing that Market Biofeedback dictates how they adapt and change as a trader. By simply acknowledging Market Biofeedback, you can understand how you react to the market in general, and how your trades, in particular, mold your approach to trading. Market Biofeedback is the one area that most traders neglect, most traders are not quite aware of this process. By paying attention to Market Biofeedback over time, you will be able to become aware of, and eventually control your trading behaviors. This will allow you to take a big step towards consistent profits.

If you would like to learn more about Market Biofeedback, please go to www.marketbiofeedback.com.

CHAPTER 3

Back-Testing Your System

You need to continue to gain expertise, but avoid thinking like an expert.

—Denis Waitley

The consistently profitable forex trader is an expert. Just as an expert farmer understands seeds and soil, and the expert mechanic can hear the difference between a blown gasket and loose muffler, the expert forex trader knows markets. Where does this expertise come from? How does the novice forex trader become an expert? This is the million-dollar question.

Make no mistake about it, when you step into any market, including the forex market, and decide that you want to make money, you have decided you will outwit and outperform some of the most determined, intelligent, and well-resourced people in the world. All these impressive people have one goal: to take your money. How can you make money in the markets, knowing whom you are up against? The answer is simple. Perhaps the answer is much simpler that you would believe.

You must practice.

Practice your craft. Practice your trading. This is the simple way to become an expert. Simple does not mean easy, because many traders expect to become experts without practice, and sadly they never achieve expertise. Consistently profitable trading is yours if you practice trading and become an expert.

You now have the secret formula to achieve consistently profitable trading. Will you use this secret? The best estimates suggest as many as 74.8 percent of traders do not use the secret. This is because 74.8 percent of forex traders do not consistently make money trading (*Forex Magnates U.S. Forex Brokers Profitability Report for Quarter 2*, 2011). The 25.2 percent of consistently profitable traders practice trading to get better at it.

Only 25.2 percent of all of the traders reading this will decide to practice trading to become an expert. It is no coincidence that about 25.2 percent of all traders are consistently profitable. Practice helps achieve expertise in nearly every sport and vocation. It is interesting to see how the vast majority of aspiring traders expect to immediately become successful without putting the effort into *becoming* an expert.

Expert traders put the effort into becoming an expert. It is ironic that many traders are attracted to the trading lifestyle, thinking that trading will allow passive income to accumulate. This is certainly true, any trader can make money while sleeping, but expert traders are much more likely to achieve consistent, passive income from trading. Trading is like any other job: Practice and effort must be well-placed in order to reap the rewards. The expert trader may be able to quickly make trading decisions and place trades, but these decisions are the fruits of many hours of practice, in nearly every instance. Traders must *earn* their pips through practice.

Practice means confidence. Practicing your trading system will enable you to keep trading your system, and avoid all distractions and excuses (e.g., terrible-system traders and bad-market traders) along the way. Practicing your trading system will allow you to enjoy the confidence of knowing when you place a trade how likely you are to be successful with that particular trade.

Would you enjoy trading more if you had a quiet, unshakable confidence in your trading system? Would you find it easier to walk away from your computer if you knew the precise likelihood that your trade would be a winner? Would it be nice to know that you will avoid the excuses bad-market traders and terrible-system traders make? What would happen if, from today onward, you maintained confidence in your ability to extract profits from the market even through the ups and downs that are inevitable in any trader's life?

Consistently profitable traders, otherwise known as expert traders, have one thing in common: They test their trading systems. These traders *practice* their trading systems. There are many methods for testing a trading system. Each of them has advantages and disadvantages.

Depending on your personality and how you approach your trading, one of these approaches is likely to resonate with you more than the others. Decide which of the three methods you will adopt to become an expert trader.

Each of these methods are back-testing methods. *Back-testing* is a common term used in trading that simply means "testing a trading system through historical data." All traders know that using historical data is not the perfect solution to testing a trading system. A much better alternative would be to have future data to test our trading systems. Failing that, historical data is the next best thing. There are many pitfalls and problems associated with testing trading systems on historical data; however, the consequences associated with trading a system in live market conditions when it is *not tested on historical data* are much more problematic.

THREE GOALS OF BACK-TESTING

Your back-testing will allow you to do two things: First, you will identify how suitable the trading system is for you. This does not mean you are discovering whether the trading system is profitable, but, rather, you are examining the fit between you, the trader, and the rules of your trading system. Second, you will learn to *trust* your trading system and learn to let go of your trades. You may trade in a more relaxed manner once you have taken thousands of trades over years of market data. The confidence gained by trading your system repeatedly will show up in the form of a relaxed approach to your live trading. Third, you will gain expertise with your trading system. This may only happen if you take many trades, and back-testing is a quick way to accumulate many trades. A close look at each of these three goals may help you to get the most out of your back-testing.

Is the System Suitable?

How suitable is your trading system? The first goal of back-testing is to find out how suitable the trading system is for you. I have a good friend, who introduced me to forex, named Ashkan Bolour. Bolour is a well-known forex trader, you may have read about him in the *Millionaire Traders* book by Kathy Lien and Boris Schlossberg. Bolour trades the three-minute and five-minute charts. He does exceptionally well trading these charts. No matter how many times I watch him trade his systems on these charts, I always fail when I try to trade as he does. I fail because his trading system does not *fit* with my view of the markets. I prefer the daily, weekly, and four-hour charts. I have great difficulty watching my trades fluctuate, which is precisely what Bolour does when he trades. I have learned to trade systems that make sense to me. I am better at extracting profits from the longer-term charts. Your job is to find out how you should be trading, and trade only what makes sense to you.

Perhaps you have traded several trading systems in the past. Most of these systems probably looked outstanding at first glance. Maybe you paid for the trading system, and the website you bought it from painted the system as an invincible profit-collecting machine. Or maybe you read about the system on an Internet forum. Or perhaps a friend told you about the trading system. No matter how good the trading system appears, it is remarkable how *your trading results* often differ from your expectations of the system. How can a perfect, profitable system fall apart in your hands? Why is it that a system that sounds good does not work once you start trading it?

The answer is *fit*; if a system does not fit your view of the markets, your approach to trading, your ability to execute trades, it will not make money for you. A system must fit with your understanding of the markets. If you believe the five-minute chart is "random noise," you may be better suited to trade the daily chart. If you believe moving averages are useless indicators, you will not be comfortable with a moving-average-based system. If you think that the USD/JPY is a terrible pair to trade, you are not going to trade a system on the USD/JPY. Your beliefs about trading must fit your trading system.

Your lifestyle will also determine the types of systems you may trade. If you have a full-time job, and spend 10 hours of the day at an office where you will not have access to your trading platform, you probably will be drawn toward longer-term charts. Daily, weekly, or four-hour charts may be best for you. This way, you may take your trades and manage them by checking the charts once or twice each day.

Your makeup as a trader will also determine how you should trade. Perhaps you freak out when you are in a trade on the lower-timeframe charts, such as the five-minute charts. Perhaps it is torture watching the profit and loss fluctuate greatly with each pip gained or lost on these lower-timeframe charts. If this is the case, you will probably want to trade higher-timeframe charts. If you are risking the same percentage of your account on each trade, it is likely that a trade on a lower timeframe chart will risk more per pip because the stop loss is closer to the entry price than a trade on a higher-timeframe chart. Your back-testing experience with the trading system will show you whether you will be able to find profits with a system. Testing will also show you whether your lifestyle will fit with the system. Perhaps most of the trade signals for a trading system occur during the European market, and you are fast asleep during that time; this may mean that the trading system is not for you.

Confidence Is Letting Go

After you have found a system that fits your personality, your view of the markets, you need to get comfortable trading this system. This will be the second step you take on your way to consistent profits in forex. The key here is to gain experience over a broad range of market conditions. Relaxing while you are in a trade will often help you *manage* the trade better. Just the simple fact that you are relaxed means your decision-making will be better.

Relaxation will come for you once you have confidence in your system, a confidence gained by trading your system repeatedly, over years of market conditions and a variety of signals. You will learn to *trust* your trading system and learn to let go of your trades. Micromanaging trades, particularly trades on higher timeframes, is a common mistake of novice traders. If you can walk away from your computer after making a trade, you have confidence in your system. This confidence is only available to traders who have back-tested extensively.

Accelerate your learning curve by back-testing. It does not matter your method of back-testing; it only matters that you *do it*. Testing over thousands of trades will enable you to be better prepared to make a decision on your trading system. Once you deem your system profitable, you can begin to get comfortable with the system by testing extensively, slowly building your database of trading experience with the system. Your next step will be to become an expert with your system.

You Are the Expert

The number-one reason traders fail in forex is this: Most traders do not have expertise. Most traders begin trading a system without much experience trading a system. When the first bump in the road appears (e.g. an extended losing period, a lack of signals for a week, a couple of difficult-to-interpret signals, etc.) the system is abandoned. The traders who consistently pull profits from the market are experts, without exception.

To become an expert at anything, you must do it at least 10,000 times. If you want to become an expert in your chosen trading system, you *could* take 10,000 trades, which will probably take you years to achieve, or you could back-test your system. By seriously testing your system over thousands of trades, you will quickly achieve expertise with your system. Seriously testing your system means making trades just as you would with your live account: trading from the right-hand edge of the chart, without the benefit of hindsight bias, using a strict application of your trading rules.

The naked trader has an advantage over traders who trade "normal," indicator-based systems. A trader who is trading a system incorporating seven indicators must view and interpret all seven indicators for each trade, before, during, and after every signal is initiated. This is cumbersome and slow. The naked trader has a chart with no indicators, a very clean chart. These charts are easy to interpret. In fact, the naked trader gains experience with his system every time he sees a chart in a newspaper, on television, in a book, regardless of market. This is because the naked trader can see, at a glance, whether the chart suggests a buy signal, a sell signal, or no trade signal. A chart on the nightly news helps the naked trader march toward expertise. In this way, the naked trader has a distinct advantage over traders using indicators. Expertise will come more quickly, more easily, and allow the naked trader to interpret any chart, in any market, at any time.

Experts in cognitive psychology agree that experts at the highest level find it difficult to teach their expertise. Experts know what to do, in fact, because their expert behavior is automatic. They do not *think* about what they do, they just do it. Novices spend a lot of time thinking about the procedures, setting things up correctly, and so forth. Experts spend time thinking about *how they interpret information*—a very different approach.

So what does this mean for your trading? It means you should backtest extensively. Your goal should be to pull out of the novice trader stage and into the expert level as quickly as possible. The fast way to achieve expertise is to gain experience trading your system via testing. All novice traders spend a good proportion of time in orientation, "Is this a good signal?" "Does this set-up qualify as a valid trade set-up?" "Should I take this trade? I am not sure if this constitutes a good signal ..." Expert traders spend more time evaluating the trade once it is initiated. In other words, experts are concerned with Market Biofeedback, and novice traders are concerned with understanding the system rules. This is understandable, novice traders spend time thinking about possible trade set-ups, novice traders are still learning the trading system. Expert traders spend more time *managing* trades and focusing on making sure that open trades are managed efficiently, to extract maximum profits from the market once those profits become available.

One of the true paradoxes of expertise is this: Experts find it difficult to verbalize the decision-making process. Expert traders are often unable to adequately explain how to duplicate their results. This is frustrating for the novice. Experts often rely on unconscious thinking, or a "gut feeling" when making decisions. The subtle cues experts use to make a decision are ingrained and rote, often inaccessible to conscious consideration, and this is frustrating for novice traders who are seeking expertise. Novice traders are better off spending time gaining experience through testing, building toward expertise, rather than trying to find a shortcut to expertise by mirroring experts.

Unless you want to allow a computer to do all the trading for you—in other words you trade only fully automated trading systems—you probably will want to achieve trading expertise. Your shortcut to trading expertise is to back-test. Although it may seem like hard work, the fact is you can simply accumulate years of experience over hours when you decide to manually back-test. It is, quite simply, the best shortcut to trading success. The very successful traders, who are consistently finding profits in the market, who are trading for a living, all of them share one characteristic: They back-test their systems and earn their pips on their back-testing software. Why not join this successful group of traders today?

MANUAL BACK-TESTING

Manual back-testing is the most readily available form of back-testing available. Most traders understand it is possible to manually back-test their trading systems, but most traders choose not to manually back-test. Many charting packages make it easy to back-test. The vast majority of charts will allow the historical price, so that you may advance price slowly and "trade" the chart as it unfolds. For example, in Meta Trader™ you simply hit the F12 key on your keyboard to advance the charts one price bar at a time. This is all that is needed for manual back-testing.

CANDLESTICK

The candlestick is a popular chart that displays the opening price, the closing price, the high price and the low price for a market during a given time period. Each candlestick clearly represents the important market activity for the given time period.

To manually back-test, you simply scroll back in time and record your trades, the trades you *would have* taken had you been trading the chart in live market conditions. You can advance the candlesticks slowly, one at a time, record your entry price, the number of lots traded, your stop loss, and your profit target. You may be concerned that manual back-testing involves a lot of notes, spreadsheets, and recordkeeping. It is a meticulous, involved, and laborious method of back-testing. It is also extremely powerful. If you aspire to trade by looking at a chart and making a trading decision, you are nearly duplicating the trading process with this form of back-testing.

Most traders employ discretionary trading systems, so it follows that manual back-testing is the most appropriate form of back-testing for most traders.

Obviously manual back-testing will take some time, and it is sometimes difficult to avoid "cheating" with this type of back-testing. However, you must take care to avoid going forward on the chart and then reversing back in time to take a trade you would have taken. The key is to trade as if you are in that moment in time, with no information of the future. The experience gained with manual back-testing is priceless. You can quickly accumulate experience with your trading system if you back-test correctly. Manual back-testing will yield statistics to help you understand the nature of your trading system. These statistics, as we will see later in this book, will become invaluable for determining how you should trade as they may be utilized to project your results into the future.

A note about manual back-testing—it may seem tedious, it will take some time, you may want to give up when it progresses slowly, particularly when you are looking to accumulate hundreds of trades. Resist the temptation to avoid manual back-testing. Make progress in small chunks, an hour of testing per day can give you a huge advantage. The payoff is great and your experience testing your system will allow you to gain "experience" trading the system through different market conditions. Each trade during manual back-testing will march you closer to expertise. This expertise may be the difference between you abandoning your trading system during the inevitable drawdown, and maintaining confidence in your trading system through a drawdown. However, there are pitfalls associated with manual back-testing.

The most common pitfall traders fall into with this testing is engaging in future trading by advancing the chart, either by accident or intention, and then deciding that a trade *would have* been taken. Traders at times have difficulty discerning when future price data creeps into manual back-testing. Traders who are strict about not allowing trades after future data is viewed will avoid contaminating back-testing data. By trading only from the current candlestick on the chart, serious back-testers avoid going forward in time.

Hindsight bias is a critical killer that may creep into your manual back-testing if you allow it to happen. A good rule of thumb is to advance the charts slowly during your testing, and if you accidentally advance the chart too quickly, you must keep your trades to the right-hand edge of the chart. If you advance the chart and then go back to take a trade, you are leaving yourself open to the hindsight bias.

HINDSIGHT BIAS

The tendency to overestimate the predictability of the market *after the future outcome is known.*

Even if you only take trades during testing by advancing the chart one candlestick at a time, hindsight bias may still sneak into your testing. If you are testing historical data on the EUR/USD in 2008, and you had experience trading in 2008, you may have a problem. Your *subconscious* may be pulling up the 2008 EUR/USD chart and you are obviously not even aware of it. To fight hindsight bias, take trades on the right-hand edge of the chart, do not go forward on the chart and then reverse back, and if you do accidentally go forward, resign yourself to skipping over any signals that pop up and stick to trading on the right-hand edge of the chart.

USING BACK-TESTING SOFTWARE

Back-testing software is a step up from manual back-testing. Most forex traders are not even aware of the fact that manually back-testing your trading system is possible. Back-testing software is an underappreciated tool, one that will allow you to manually back-test your trading system at an aggressive pace. Manual back-testing software records your trades for you and enables you to quickly take trades as you advance the historical charts. In many ways, manual back-testing with software is not much different from manual back-testing. The advantages to using software are as follows: Software will allow faster testing, so you may accumulate experience quicker; the software will do the recordkeeping for you and allow you to concentrate on the trade signals; you may easily export your data for analysis; and software discourages cheating— manual back-testing software is a hindsight bias killer.

Of the many manual back-testing software packages available, my favorite is Forex Tester. Forex Tester is a manual back-testing software package that will allow you to import any data. You may decide to import forex data, futures data, stock data—any data will work. Forex tester will record your trades and allow you to export your trading data into a spreadsheet, after you have completed your testing, for analysis. The beauty of software-based testing is that it allows you to concentrate on trading your system. In many ways, it mirrors live trading with an account platform. If you would like to see a video demonstration of Forex Tester please go to www.fxjake.com/book.

There are many traders, myself included, who will spend more time back-testing with software because it is much easier than manual back-testing. Back-testing with software helps traders gain years of trading experience in a few hours. However, the real work in back-testing is examining the results. Exporting and analyzing the data from back-testing is where serious traders validate trading systems, find behavioral patterns, and develop strategies to augment profitable trading strategies. These data are gold for the serious trader.

Your back-testing data will help you determine *your* trading patterns (Do you find profits more easily on the daily charts? Are most of your winning trades initiated during the European session? Do you trade particularly well with your system on the CAD/JPY?), and this can lead to more fruitful back-testing sessions. You will also know, after back-testing your system over several hundred trades, if the system makes money for you. In fact, before you ever risk one cent, you should make hundreds of trades while back-testing to verify that your trading system will capture profits and also to gain expertise with your system.

Manual back-testing with software is not without problems. You must look out for the same pitfalls that creep up with manual back-testing, namely hindsight bias. Manual back-testing software makes it easier to avoid hindsight bias, but you still must be careful to only take trades if you have not advanced forward on the chart. Cheating is not allowed when back-testing; your goal is to generate realistic trade results during your back-testing. Also, because it is very easy to quickly execute trades with the testing software, you must watch out for subpar trades. Trades you would not take on a live trading account should be bypassed no matter how tempting it may be to take them during back-testing. Try to back-test as if you have real money at risk. This is the only way to ensure that your statistics and experience in back-testing will closely match your live trading. If you remain vigilant and conscientious during testing, your results will be more meaningful.

AUTOMATED BACK-TESTING

Automated back-testing is the most well-known method for testing a trading system. Most forex traders are aware of the fact that it is possible to do some automated testing on a trading system. However, most forex traders use discretionary, or manual, trading systems, so automated back-testing is not the ideal method for back-testing; it does not closely duplicate the discretionary trading most traders engage in. There are many reasons for discouraging automated back-testing for discretionary traders:

- There may be too much human interpretation in the trading system. Automated back-testing does not allow for the human interpretation of trade signals.
- The trading system may involve variables that are not available on the price chart (news releases, economic data records, interpretation of world events, etc.).

- It is impossible to automate the trading system (fuzzy logic, parameters difficult to define, etc.).
- You may not be able to articulate your trading system. Automated back-testing is only possible for trading systems with clearly defined rules.

Most forex traders should not use automated back-testing. Automated back-testing is appropriate for those traders who use automated trading systems. Automated trading systems, known as trading robots, or expert advisors, are popular with forex traders. However, most traders are more comfortable with discretionary trading systems. So, while it may be possible to use automated back-testing, it may not be appropriate for most traders.

Here is a test to help you decide whether automated back-testing is for you. If you turn on your automated trading system and can allow it to trade without any of your intervention for a month, then automated back-testing may be for you. If your system needs your input for any reason, then you are a discretionary trader, and you should use manual back-testing or manual back-testing with software.

There are other disadvantages to automated back-testing. It does not allow you to gain experience with the trading system. You will not gain the expertise that you would if you manually tested the system because the computer takes all of the trades over the course of the back-testing. Automated back-testing will not give you experience trading your system through many market conditions. Automated back-testing will probably not highlight the weaknesses of your trading system; these weaknesses will be readily apparent when manual back-testing is done. However, with automated back-testing, the weaknesses are a bit more difficult to identify. In short, automated back-testing is really only an option for those traders who are not using a discretionary trading system.

There are unique pitfalls associated with automated back-testing. For example, it is quite easy to use too many variables in an automated trading system. Using too many variables often implies that there are too many indicators in the trading system. Seasoned traders understand how simple trading systems are robust, and may be applied to many markets over varying timeframes. (All of the naked-trading systems in this book are incredibly simple and robust.) It is difficult for some automated-system developers to keep their trading systems simple and robust; the temptation to add more indicators and rules is great.

It is exceptionally easy for automated traders to use too many indicators when developing and testing a system. Adding too many variables to any trading system increases the chances that the trading system will work quite well on one data set but will not work well on another. With too many variables the system is likely to do exceptionally well during some market conditions and then break down and perform poorly when market conditions change. This is a very real risk with automated back-testing. It is almost too easy for a trader to decide to add more conditions and indicators to the trading system, which will increase the profitability of the trading system over the course of the historical data in the back-test, often making the system look very good. However, these results often completely fall apart after you apply this very same trading system to a different data set or to future market conditions. In a very real sense, the Achilles heel of automated back-testing is that it is too easy. Because the automated back-tests can be generated so quickly, the automated back-tester will go overboard tweaking and testing the system. The end result is often a system that works *exceptionally well* on the historical data in the back-test but falls apart completely in live market conditions.

There is another issue that often comes up with automated back-testing. This is the postdictive error, a fancy way of saying that a trading system uses future information to make a decision in the present time. This is actually something that is related to the hindsight bias. Traders back-testing automated trading systems must be extremely careful. It is possible for the back-tester to pull data from the future without knowing about it. This is obviously a very big problem, because as a rule, future data is not generally available, despite any claims to the contrary by technical indicator salespeople (psychics and palm readers are the obvious exceptions). When future data is used in an automated back-test, the system looks incredible, but once the trading system is applied to real market conditions, without the critical (future) data, the system falls apart.

There is one advantage to automated back-testing, that is, it allows you to quickly determine whether an automated trading strategy is viable. The back-test may be done in seconds, which is a true advantage for the automated trader. Remember, the automated trader will not gain the same expertise and comfort level as the trader who uses manual back-testing. This is the biggest weakness of automated back-testing, the back-tests are cheap. There is no experience gained each time a back-test is run. The manual back-testing trader accumulates experience every time a trade set-up is executed. This experience should not be discounted. An automated back-test may clarify the worthiness of an automated trading system, often involving hundreds, or thousands of trades, but remember the trades are all taken by computer and will not lead to trader expertise. In this sense the trades are wasted, the trader does not accumulate experience during the back-testing, this is only possible with manual back-testing.

If you use automated trading systems, then, perhaps, automated back-testing is appropriate, but if you use manual trading systems, it may be best to avoid automated back-testing.

TOP THREE BACK-TESTING TIPS

There is one distinguishing characteristic between those traders who continually struggle to find consistent profits and those traders who consistently pull profits from the market. The traders who are still looking for consistency, who are still looking for profits, are traders who usually do not back-test trading systems. These traders fall in love with a system before establishing the veracity of the system. These traders often move from trading system to trading system, hoping that the new system will yield better results than the previous system. The consistently profitable traders take a different approach. These traders *know* that they have a profitable system because they back-test their system extensively. These traders have seen their system work over years of market data and know precisely the type of drawdown they are likely to come up against in the future.

The choice is yours; you may decide to join the group of struggling traders who jump from system to system, never really finding comfort with any trading system, or you may decide to join the successful traders, the profitable group who spend time back-testing their systems. If you decide to join the latter group, I have three back-testing tips for you. These tips were developed by working with traders just like you, around the world. The key is to approach your back-testing as you would any skill you are working toward. If you were looking to learn the bass guitar, you would probably want to take lessons and spend time playing your guitar to hone your skills. However, it is important that you play the bass guitar in *your* own style. Back-testing is much the same. You must approach it seriously, but you must also keep this in mind: You will consistently find profits only if you stay true to your trading style.

Consider Your Style

Use a back-testing method that fits your trading style. If you are an automated trader, then use automated back-testing; if you are a discretionary trader, use manual back-testing. The most important thing in back-testing is to duplicate your trading style. Back-test in a way that will be meaningful and bring you closer to expertise with your system.

Take Time to Test

There is a real temptation, particularly when engaging in manual back-testing with software, to do it much too quickly. Back-testing is a learning process. Just as you would not expect to complete a 16-week course in a day, you will need to break up your back-testing sessions, particularly if you are doing manual back-testing. Try to keep your sessions short—under two hours—so that you approach each session with a fresh mind and you are unlikely to get sloppy. Back-testing for six or more hours will usually lead to poor results simply because you were not as sharp for your last trades as you were for your first trades.

Mistakes Are Part of Back-Testing

Making mistakes is also part of the learning process. We have a natural tendency to avoid mistakes. So when a trading mistake pops up several times, it is tempting to modify the trading system so that it accounts for this mistake. However, this is the road that leads to too many variables in a trading system. Avoid too many variables. Try to keep your system rules simple. It may be tempting to add a new rule to avoid some losing trades, but this may blunt the effectiveness of your system.

If you are interested in naked trading, trading without indicators, then you are likely to avoid the "too many rules" mistake. This is another reason why naked trading allows traders to realize their full potential.

Naked trading also involves using the history of the market. If you ask any psychologist how to best learn about someone, you will hear that it is best to follow that person around. Psychologists do not have the time to follow people around, so questionnaires are used to determine what somebody is like—their personality, their habits, and their history. Likewise, the naked trader may use the history of the market to determine what is likely to happen in the future. Everyone has done something and said, "Why do I do that?" People like to believe in free choice, but most humans are creatures of habit. Likewise, the market is a huge amalgamation of habitual traders. The market is nothing more than a community of creatures of habit. People make up the market. The naked trader uses this to his advantage, by closely following historical turning points in the market. We will get into this issue in detail later in the book, but for now it is important to remember that the naked trader equates the market to a herd. Herds will often follow one another for safety. Members of a herd will also fall on one another as they run off a cliff. The naked trader uses specific tools to tune into and take advantage of the herd behavior that we call the market.

CHAPTER 4

Identifying Support and Resistance Zones

There's an old saying about those who forget history.
I don't remember it, but it's good.

—Stephen Colbert

Y ou have to pay close attention to one thing on the chart if you trade naked: price. Price is king. Price will tell you all you need to know. The wonderful thing that all markets have is this: a history. The market will tell you where the sweet spot is on the chart. These sweet spots will be the foundation for everything you do as a naked trader.

A sweet spot on the chart is a support and resistance zone. You may be familiar with the concept of support and resistance, however, support and resistance zones are different from what many traders characterize as support and resistance. I will call these support and resistance zones by one word— *zones*. The eight important characteristics of zones are as follows:

1. Zones are an area, not a price point.
2. Zones are like fine wine; they get better with age.
3. Zones are spots on the chart where price reverses, repeatedly.
4. Zones may be extreme highs or lows on the chart.
5. Zones are where naked traders find trading opportunities.
6. Support and resistance zones rarely need to be modified.
7. Line charts help naked traders find zones.
8. Zones are often seen by many traders.

You may want to take a closer look at each of these eight characteristics. It is incredibly important that you understand how to draw zones, why you should draw zones on your charts, and understand when these zones become critical for your trading.

ZONES ARE BIG FAT BEER BELLIES

A zone is simply a big fat beer belly. Many traders have misconceptions concerning zones. Traders may be familiar with the concept of support and resistance but unfortunately, many misapply this concept to technical trading. The naked trader understands that zones are an *area* on the chart. This is a very distinct concept to a support and resistance *line*. A support and resistance line indicates a specific price on the chart, but zones are something different. Zones are not a specific price. These zones are, instead, an area, a range, or, as I prefer, a beer belly.

Let me explain. I prefer to think of these zones on the chart as if they were beer bellies. Before you disregard this idea, consider what a beer belly is: A beer belly is somewhat firm, maybe somewhat repulsive, and has some predictable characteristics. My friend Jason has a beer belly. He is quite proud of it; he tells me it is quite expensive, as he has paid good money for the wine and beer that have enabled him to grow this belly. If I were to push into Jason's beer belly with my fist (I would never push into a beer belly without permission, and I suggest you, too, first obtain permission before pushing any beer bellies), eventually I would find resistance. Even if at first I did not find resistance, eventually there would be a point at which the squishy beer belly would stop me from pushing further. This is a critical characteristic, for I know that I may be able to push a little bit into the beer belly, but eventually the beer belly will offer some resistance.

Perhaps you may also decide to push into Jason's beer belly with your fist. You may have a different experience. Perhaps, when you start to push into Jason's beer belly, you become somewhat unsettled and decide to pull back after only slightly brushing the hair covering his beer belly. This is completely reasonable, and I am sure that many others will have the same reaction. However, the important thing to note here is that you and I are pushing into the same beer belly, Jason's beer belly, but we find resistance at different spots on the beer belly.

This is a significant feature of zones. Zones are just like beer bellies. Zones are spots on the chart where price has pushed and probed, and then reversed. Naked traders love beer bellies. They love these zones. Naked traders wait for price to reach these zones before initiating a trade. The zone is the sweet spot on the chart for the naked trader. It is absolutely critical that the naked trader identifies the zones on the chart. These zones are the foundation of naked trading.

OLD ZONES, NEW ZONES

The age of zones, and the importance of the age of a zone, is a hotly debated topic among traders. Some traders believe that only those zones that have been established recently are important, and other traders believe that zones that were established long ago are just as important as the newly minted zones. I believe that zones are recycled.

If you take a look at any chart for any currency, you will find historical price levels. What you will notice is that price has a tendency to reverse at the same levels repeatedly. This is a distinguishing trait of zones, and you may use this characteristic to define and discover zones on your currency charts.

Hot Pizza and Zones

When I was a young child, at about six, I used to watch my mother in the kitchen. It was fun. In fact, some of my very first memories are of my mother singing to me in the kitchen. One day, while in the kitchen, I had a terrible accident. On this day my mother was baking pizza, and it smelled delicious. In fact, you may find it hard to believe, but to this day I still love pizza. My mother was busy chopping up the ingredients for the pizza, making the sauce, because she had several pizzas to make. I wandered over to the first pizza. It was still on a hot pan because it had only just been removed from the oven.

Now, my mother had warned me to be wary of the hot pizza pan. I had either forgotten or disregarded her warning, and I decided to grab the pizza pan because the pizza smelled so good. As you may imagine, I completely burned my hand. I still remember it being extremely painful and still have the scars.

I learned a lesson that day. I still love pizza, but I am wary of hot pans. It was a valuable lesson I learned, and is something that I think about every time I look at a currency pair on the chart, I think about that pizza day. Every time I see a chart approaching a zone, I consider that the market may remember the last time it was burnt at that price level, at that zone.

Do Zones = Market Scars?

Take a look at the Figure 4.1. This is the daily chart for the EUR/CAD currency pair. Note that this pair found support at the critical level of 1.4350

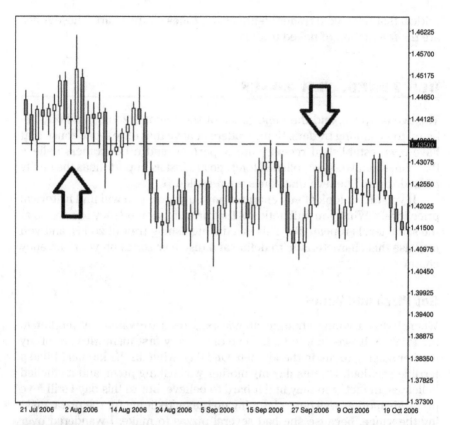

FIGURE 4.1 Support/Resistance Zone on the EUR/CAD Daily Chart in 2006. The market finds support in July and August 2006 at 1.4350, and then in September and October of 2006 the market finds resistance on the very same zone at 1.4350.
© 2000–2011, MetaQuotes Software Corp.

back in July and August of 2006 (up arrow). The pair repeatedly found support at this level over many weeks. Then, in September and October of 2006, the pair trades back to this zone and finds resistance on three separate occasions at the 1.4350 level (down arrow).

Now take a look at the next chart, same pair, the EUR/CAD in Figure 4.2. Here the pair has found resistance back up at the 1.4350 level, *four years later.* The market moves back to this critical 1.4350 level, finds resistance there and promptly falls. The chart has a memory! This is a very clear zone for this currency pair. Do you think that knowing where price may turn around is an advantage for you, as a naked trader?

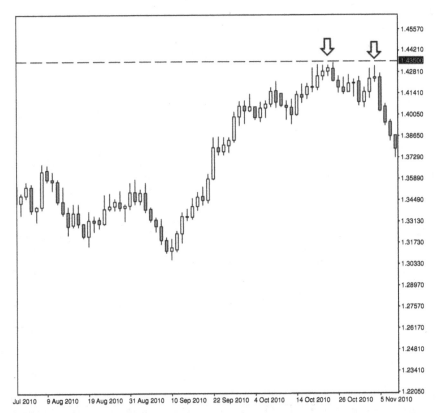

FIGURE 4.2 Support/Resistance Zone on the EUR/CAD Daily Chart in 2010. After trading higher and higher, the market finds resistance at the 1.4350 zone and price falls lower.
© 2000–2011, MetaQuotes Software Corp.

Perhaps you may be thinking that other markets do not have a memory for zones. Maybe this EUR/CAD example is just an exception rather than the rule. If you are thinking this, please take a few moments to look at a few charts for yourself. Another example in Figure 4.3, this is the USD/CHF daily chart from July 2008. Notice how the market came down and touched the 1.000 zone (arrow) and then rocketed higher.

Over a year later, in 2009 the USD/CHF falls back down to the same 1.0000 level and finds support on three occasions, as you can see in Figure 4.4. The market traded sharply higher after the third touch on the 1.0000 zone. Again, the market has made a critical reversal at a price that has

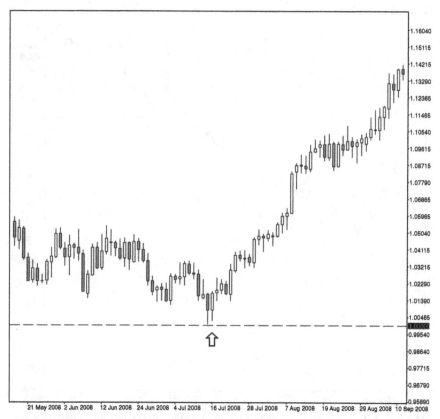

FIGURE 4.3 The USD/CHF daily chart shows a distinct zone at the 1.0000 where the market finds support in 2008.
© 2000–2011, MetaQuotes Software Corp.

historically served as a turning point. This is what zones are, historical turning points.

Another example is shown in Figure 4.5. This time it is the EUR/USD daily chart. In 2003 this pair topped out at 1.1930, there were several touches on this zone (see three arrows).

Years later the EUR/USD was freefalling from a high of over 1.5100 and the pair eventually found support 3000 pips lower, on a very critical zone (see Figure 4.6). The 1.1930 level served as critical support seven years later. The chart has a memory!

These zones are critical for the naked trader; once price reaches a zone, the naked trader is on alert for a possible trade set-up. Why would the naked trader want to know once price reaches a zone? Because price has

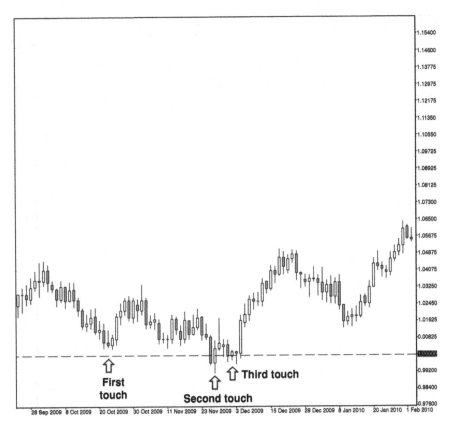

FIGURE 4.4 In 2009, the USD/CHF again finds support on the critical 1.0000 zone.
© 2000–2011, MetaQuotes Software Corp.

repeatedly turned around at these zones! Knowing what a market has done in the past is critical for the naked trader, not because the naked trader *assumes* the market will turn around again, but because the naked trader is on high alert, and the market *may* turn around again. Some traders are literally on alert, if you would like to see a free video on how you can set up price alerts so that your charts send you an e-mail when price reaches a zone, go to www.fxjake.com/book.

The naked trader does not take trades based on price reaching a zone, the naked trader uses several tools to decide when to take a trade. However, the naked trader will not take a trade unless price has reached a zone. This is the first step (price reaching a zone) for the naked trader, when setting up a trade.

FIGURE 4.5 The daily EUR/USD has a clear zone at the 1.1930 level in 2003. The market finds resistance three times in quick succession.
© 2000–2011, MetaQuotes Software Corp.

HOW TO FIND ZONES

Zones are those spots on the chart where price has repeatedly reversed. However, it may be difficult at first for you to find these zones on the chart. There are several sneaky shortcuts that you can use to help develop an eye for finding zones. Some zones are extremely obvious and easy to find. Other zones are a little bit trickier and may be difficult for you to identify if you have not had experience finding zones on the chart. Please keep in mind these three shortcuts when you are drawing your zones on the chart.

1. Start with a higher timeframe chart.
2. Use a line chart to find the zones on the chart.
3. Ignore minor zones.

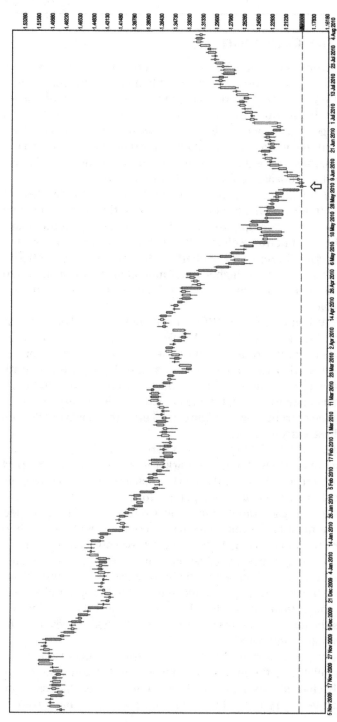

FIGURE 4.6 The daily EUR/USD falls over 3000 pips and eventually finds support at the 1.1930 zone in 2010, seven years after first finding resistance on this zone.

© 2000–2011, MetaQuotes Software Corp.

Use a Higher Timeframe Chart

Question: When you meet someone new, how do you decide what they are like? You learn their history, you ask people about them, you try and decipher what they have done in the past, in the hopes of understanding them better. Why do you do this? The implicit assumption is that they will do the same things they have done in the past *in the future*. Markets are no different. When the market is on a runaway uptrend, traders look to the older charts to see where the critical zones are on the chart. This is also where we see history repeat itself, over and over and over again.

This shortcut for finding zones on the chart will work regardless of the timeframe you are trading. Simply move up one timeframe. This is a very powerful method for finding the most important zones on the chart. Examining the higher timeframe chart will enable you to identify zones that will be the most critical areas on the chart for the timeframe you choose to trade. A few touches on the higher timeframe chart will translate into many touches on the lower timeframe chart. This technique will work on any timeframe chart.

Take a look at Figure 4.7, the GBP/USD one-hour chart. This pair has made an extreme low at the 1.6291 level. This touch at 1.6291 suggests the market has made a significant low, and this level may become important later. You may recall that extreme touches (lows or highs) are also critical zones. Although most zones will have touches from above and below (support and resistance touches), touches at extreme levels are also very critical, such as the extreme low in Figure 4.7. Later, the market will often come back to these extreme levels.

A month later, the GBP/USD *four*-hour chart (Figure 4.8) suggests two very interesting conclusions. First, the market *has* indeed found support and resistance on the 1.6291 level; the market has a memory. Second, the four-hour chart shows a very *clear* perspective for this market.

Moving up to a higher timeframe is an excellent way to gain perspective. Only the most important zones will become evident on a higher-timeframe chart. If you are using Meta Trader™ for your charts, you will have the following time frames available: one minute, five minutes, 15 minutes, 30 minutes, one hour, four hours, daily, weekly, and monthly. Thus, if you are trading the one-hour chart, a move up to the four-hour chart will help to identify the critical zones. The GBP/USD zone at 1.6291 is clearly a critical zone, as the market touches this zone more than six times over the course of one month (Figure 4.8).

This brings up an important point about zones. The importance of a zone is directly related to the number of touches on that zone. So, for instance, if a daily chart shows a zone with five touches over the past year, this would indicate a very critical zone on that particular chart. Here is

FIGURE 4.7 The 1.6291 level on the GBP/USD one-hour chart appears to be an extreme low, so a zone is assumed at this level.
© 2000–2011, MetaQuotes Software Corp.

another example: Notice on Figure 4.9, the EUR/CAD daily chart, that the 1.4350 zone has served as resistance three times over two months.

Moving back a bit further, we see in Figure 4.10 that the 1.4350 area was an area of resistance seven months prior to the recent touches on the zone.

If we go back even further, we can see in Figure 4.11 how there are many touches on this very same zone, the 1.4350 zone, as price has found both support and resistance on this zone. These touches occurred on this very same critical area, the 1.4350 area, almost five *years* prior.

Some traders will say that old zones no longer matter. Traders say things like "things have changed," or "with inflation these old levels do not mean as much anymore," or "why would the market remember a level that it has not been to in over a decade?"

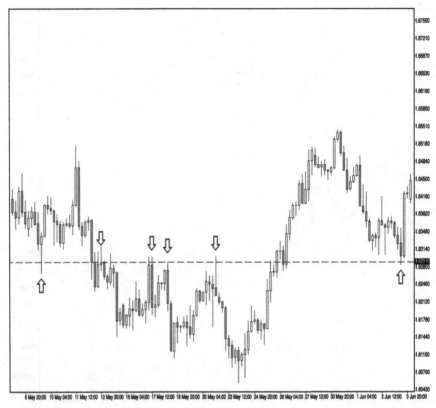

FIGURE 4.8 The market comes back to the 1.6291 zone one month later on the GBP/USD four-hour chart. Notice the repeated touches from above and below.
© 2000–2011, MetaQuotes Software Corp.

If this is currently your way of thinking, I would encourage you to take a close look at the zones on a chart 15 years ago. Just scroll back on the chart, do not consider the current price. Draw your lines on the chart based on where you find support and resistance zones 15 years ago. If your chart doesn't go back 15 years, try to go back at least 5 to 10 years. You should be able to identify critical areas on the chart from a long time ago. Now scroll forward and you will see that price in the future bounces off of these support and resistance zones. The chart has a memory. As amazing as this may sound, it is true: Price has a memory. This is true for any market, on any timeframe. I hope you go out and see this for yourself. Please do—your future as a naked trader may depend on it. The markets do remember the critical zones, this is why it is important for you, too, to remember these critical zones.

FIGURE 4.9 A Critical Zone at 1.4350 on the EUR/CAD Daily Chart.
© 2000–2011, MetaQuotes Software Corp.

The Line Chart Is Your Friend

Marking the zones on your chart is as simple as drawing a line on the chart. However, if you have not looked at charts in terms of support and resistance zones before, it may be a bit difficult to find precisely where these zones are located. It is important that, as a naked trader, you "see" these zones. One brilliant method for finding zones on the chart, and this works particularly well for those traders who are new to finding zones on the chart, is to move to a line chart. Most charting packages will allow you to view the market on a line chart. A line chart is a chart that offers a continuous line, connecting the closing prices. Rather than showing the open, the high, the low, and the close, such as a candlestick chart, or a bar chart, the line chart simply connects the closing prices.

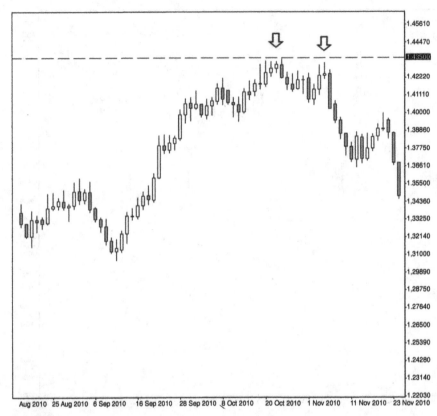

FIGURE 4.10 Seven months prior, the EUR/CAD finds resistance at the 1.4350 zone.

© 2000–2011, MetaQuotes Software Corp.

Take a look at the daily GBP/CHF chart (Figure 4.12). Where would you draw the zone?

Now, take a look at the line chart in Figure 4.13. Where would you draw the zones on this chart?

It is very obvious in Figure 4.13 that a zone should be drawn at 2.2713, and this is the beauty of the line chart. The line chart allows you to find those areas on the chart where price has "bent"—the line chart helps us to identify zones because the line chart shows where price has repeatedly bent, each bend on the line chart is a potential zone. Those places on the line chart with several bends are zones.

Line charts may also be extremely useful for those charts where price doesn't seem to be respecting a zone. Take a look at the NZD/USD

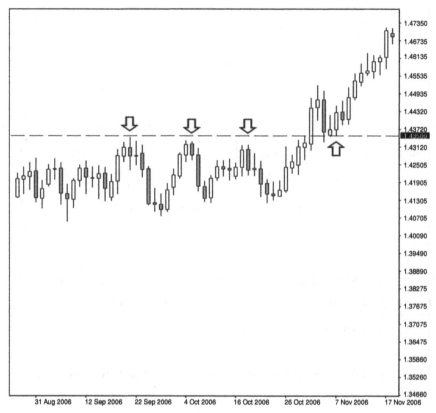

FIGURE 4.11 Nearly five years prior, the EUR/CAD repeatedly finds resistance and support at the 1.4350 zone.
© 2000–2011, MetaQuotes Software Corp.

four-hour chart in Figure 4.14. See how market prices are all over the shop and price does not seem to respect any zone? Perhaps there *is* a support and resistance zone hidden on the chart. Maybe it is there, but it is not immediately obvious *where* this zone is located.

When a chart looks like this, it may be difficult to spot the zone. Perhaps there is no zone on this chart? For these charts, the line chart may come to the rescue. A line chart may save you from sloppy price action on the charts. A line chart may make clear what is otherwise muddled and difficult to decipher. Line charts are absolutely critical for the naked trader. Notice how the price movement on the chart in Figure 4.15 becomes clear and the zone is now obvious. Because the line chart takes into

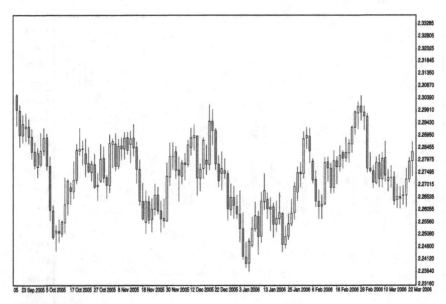

FIGURE 4.12 Sometimes zones are not very obvious, such as on this daily GBP/CHF chart.
© 2000–2011, MetaQuotes Software Corp.

consideration only the closing price, it is a very simple way to view price action.

Why the Closing Price Is Important

Now, you may wonder, "Why look at a chart that only takes into consideration the closing price?" The line chart is made up of only closing prices. This is true, but the closing prices are the most important price. It is important to note that the closing price for the forex market is usually considered the end of the North American trading session, at 5:00 P.M. New York time. Every day, there is a battle between the bulls (buyers) and bears (sellers). Traders run through the full gamut of emotions and often swing from fear to greed and back again during the trading session. However, once the end of the day approaches, traders begin to concentrate on answering this one important question: "Should I hold this trade through to tomorrow or should I close this trade now?" This is precisely why the closing price is critical, and not only in North America.

The traders in Europe also see the closing price, and may react to it. This is an important point because the closing time may be only 10:00 or

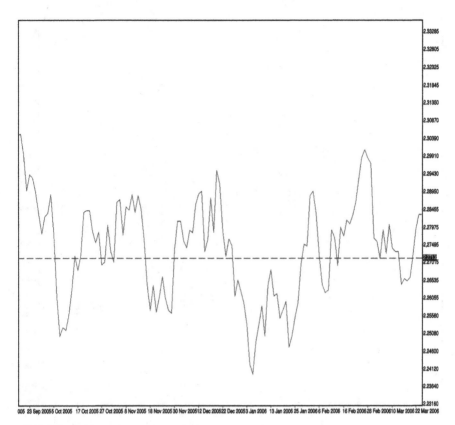

FIGURE 4.13 A line chart will often make zones easier to spot.
© 2000–2011, MetaQuotes Software Corp.

11:00 in the evening in Europe, depending on the country. Traders in the Americas and Europe spend a good portion of the day trading during the same time. This is a significant aspect of forex, because European and North American markets capture the overwhelming majority of the volume in forex. Therefore, this closing price, the last price for the New York session, is extremely important. Both traders in the Americas and the European Continent influence it. After this closing price, the market slows down considerably and shifts into the interbank market, a very slow trading period punctuated by occasional bank-to-bank transactions. In a very real sense, the North American closing price is the last price of the day before Asia wakes up and starts a new trading day.

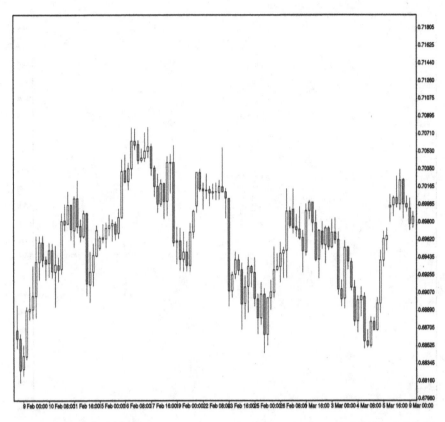

FIGURE 4.14 Sometimes zones are not very obvious. Price seems very choppy on this NZD/USD four-hour chart.
© 2000–2011, MetaQuotes Software Corp.

Zones on a Lower Time Frame Chart

You may wonder at times if a zone is important enough to draw a line on the chart. Sometimes it may not be very clear, perhaps there are a few touches on an area, but it may not be a strong area of support and resistance. If this is the case, you are probably seeing what is called a minor zone. A minor zone is nothing more than a support and resistance zone on the next-lower-timeframe chart. These zones are very apparent on the lower timeframe chart, and with practice you will spot them on the higher timeframe chart, but they are not critical areas. Marking minor zones on your chart will only make the chart confusing.

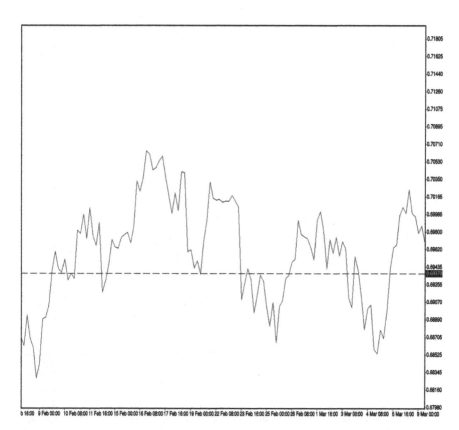

FIGURE 4.15 The line chart for the NZD/USD four-hour chart suggests a clear zone at 0.6937. Notice that there are several bends in the line chart at this zone. © 2000–2011, MetaQuotes Software Corp.

MINOR ZONES

A support and resistance zone that is apparent on the timeframe *one step lower* from the timeframe you are trading.

Later we will look at the importance of minor zones, but for now it is important to note that, although they may be apparent, they are not critical and they should not be marked on your chart. The only zones that are marked on your chart are those zones on the timeframe you are trading, and the timeframe one step higher from the chart you are trading. Any of the other zones are not important for defining your trade set ups.

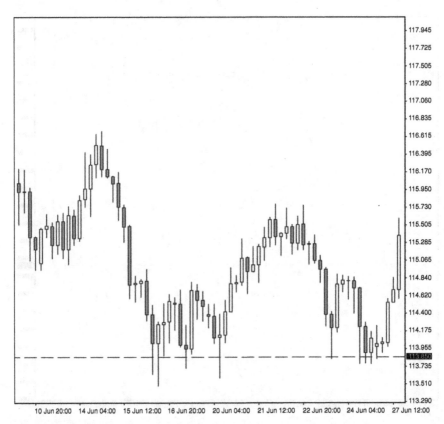

FIGURE 4.16 The four-hour EUR/JPY chart has an obvious zone at the 113.85 level.
© 2000–2011, MetaQuotes Software Corp.

In Figure 4.16, you can see an obvious zone at the 113.85 level on the EUR/JPY four-hour chart.

However, the minor zones may not be so obvious. There is also a minor zone on the EUR/JPY four-hour chart in Figure 4.17. This minor zone may be identified by the candlestick lows and the candlestick highs. It may take some practice to see these minor zones on the chart you are trading.

However, it is quite easy to see this minor zone on the EUR/JPY chart by examining a lower timeframe. Moving from the four-hour chart to the one-hour chart is one way to clearly identify this minor zone. In Figure 4.18, the minor zone on the EUR/JPY one-hour chart is clearly identified at

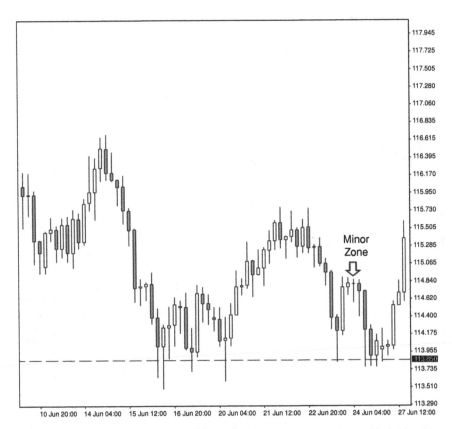

FIGURE 4.17 A minor zone on the four-hour EUR/JPY chart is marked by the arrow at 114.90. Minor zones can often be identified by candlestick highs or lows. © 2000–2011, MetaQuotes Software Corp.

114.90, the market finds support at 114.90 for several one-hour candlesticks before falling through the level, and then later, the market trades back up to 114.90 and finds resistance. This minor zone, which was difficult to see on the four-hour chart, is now easier to see because the touches from above and below are more clearly defined. Minor zones are critical for managing trades. Minor zones are hurdles, spots where price may get stuck for some time. When trading the higher timeframe chart, the only important zones are those major support and resistance zones, the standard zones.

If you find that you have too many zones drawn on your chart, then you may be identifying minor zones on your chart. Too many zones on your

FIGURE 4.18 The minor zone at 114.90 is clear to see on the one-hour EUR/JPY chart.
© 2000–2011, MetaQuotes Software Corp.

chart will mean that you will find it difficult to identify trade set-ups and profit targets for your trades. Zones may appear at any place on the chart. Some naked traders will attempt to only draw zones on the chart at round numbers, such as 1.3500 on the EUR/USD. This is not necessary. Zones may appear anywhere. If a zone is identified at 1.1097, it may be acceptable to mark it as 1.1100, but it is not necessary for all zones to fall on a round number.

Most of the time your zones will be scattered throughout your chart. Therefore, it is important to note that you may have two significant zones nearby, but in general your zones should be spread out throughout the chart (see Figure 4.19). Here are a few examples. In this chart, there are several hundred pips between zones. On a daily chart, this is common. Usually zones are separated by about 100 pips or more on a daily chart.

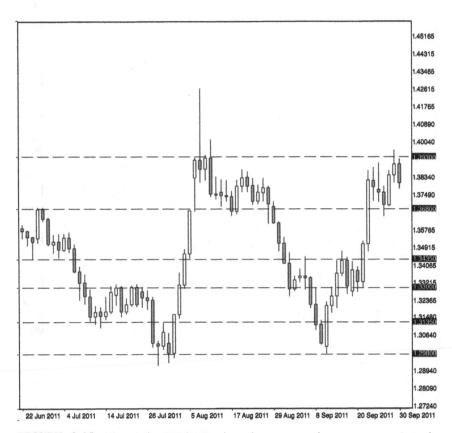

FIGURE 4.19 The daily EUR/AUD chart has zones that are approximately 100–200 pips apart.

© 2000–2011, MetaQuotes Software Corp.

The higher the time frame, the more separation between zones. Here is the EUR/USD weekly chart in Figure 4.20, and the zones are several hundred pips apart. On average, there are about 500 pips between zones.

Zones are critical for the naked trader. It is important for you to become comfortable identifying and working with zones. Zones are where the action is for the naked trader. At first you may have difficulty with zones; listed are five common trouble spots and solutions for each.

FIVE TIPS FOR FINDING ZONES

First, you may not know where to find your zones (see Figure 4.21). If you are having difficulty identifying the zones on your chart, the easiest

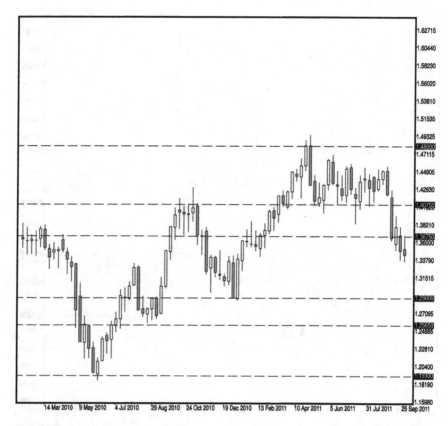

FIGURE 4.20 The weekly EUR/USD chart has zones that are about 500 pips apart.
© 2000–2011, MetaQuotes Software Corp.

solution is to simply load a line chart. The line chart will show all the zones, because the zones will be identified by the bends in the line (see Figure 4.22). At each spot where you see repeat bends in the line, you are probably looking at a zone.

Second, you may have too many zones drawn on your chart (see Figure 4.23). If you have too many zones drawn your chart, then you will probably experience two likely problems. The first problem is that you will notice many trade opportunities. If you are trading the daily chart and notice that you have a trade nearly every day, you probably have too many zones drawn on your chart. The zones should be more or less evenly spread out, and it may take some time for the market to reach these zones, and trigger a trade. Patience is important for the naked trader. Zones are critical areas on the chart, and price does not always reach these critical

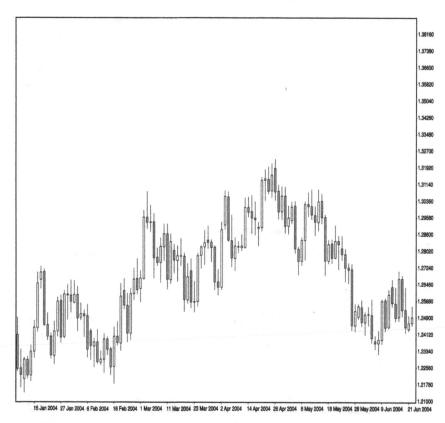

FIGURE 4.21 This is the daily USD/CHF chart. Do you see a zone on this chart? © 2000–2011, MetaQuotes Software Corp.

areas—zones—every day. The second problem that you will likely have is that you will notice many trades end up being losers. This is because the zones on your chart are not solid zones; perhaps there are minor zones identified on your chart. It is important for you to draw critical zones only, those spots in the chart where price has repeatedly reversed. By only identifying those zones on the chart where price has repeatedly reversed, the odds are in your favor. It is nearly always better to err on the side of caution. To do this, simply draw fewer zones (see Figure 4.24). If you mark only those zones on your chart where price has repeatedly reversed, you will avoid identifying the minor zones. You may miss out on some trades, but the trades you do make should be great opportunities.

The third common problem you may incur when dealing with zones is this: It often becomes very difficult to determine precisely where a zone should be drawn. This is the nature of the zone. The zone is squishy, it is fat,

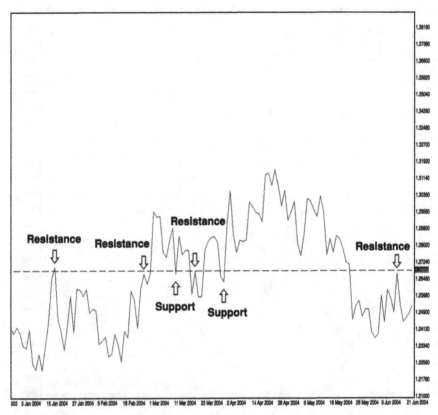

FIGURE 4.22 This is the USD/CHF daily line chart. The obvious zone at 1.2685 is now apparent. The market repeatedly finds both support and resistance on the zone.

© 2000–2011, MetaQuotes Software Corp.

it identifies an *area* on the chart, and not a specific point (see Figure 4.25). Remember that you do have some leeway in drawing your zone. It is not essential to nail down the zone to a specific price point on your chart, but rather it is important that you identify the *area* on the chart where you will look for a reversal. The touches on the zone will not be perfect. Some touches will come close to the zone, other touches will extend deep into the zone.

Notice how the 89.35 zone in Figure 4.25 has provided resistance for the daily CHF/JPY trade on several occasions. The market has fallen after reaching this zone each time, but the first two touches extended deep into the zone, and the third touch came *near* the zone. This is very common

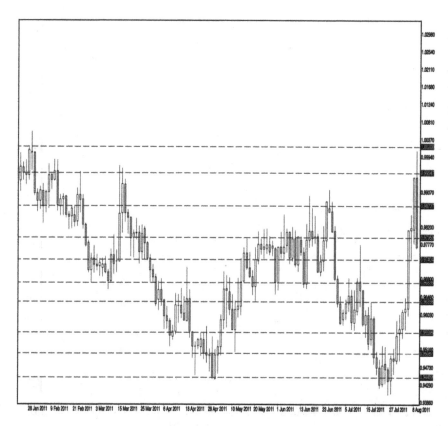

FIGURE 4.23 Too many zones are identified on this daily USD/CAD chart. The market touches a zone nearly every day on this chart because several minor zones are marked on this chart.

© 2000–2011, MetaQuotes Software Corp.

with zones; sometimes the market will brush against the beer belly and at other times the market will push into the beer belly.

The fourth problem that many traders come up against when drawing zones is that the market seems to disregard zones. When this occurs, our trusty friend the line chart can often come to the rescue. The easiest way to illustrate this issue is to take a look at an example. Take a look at this chart in Figure 4.26, and you will notice that it appears as though the market is not respecting the area at 81.83, where a zone could be drawn on the chart. However, the same chart viewed as a line chart (see Figure 4.27) shows the important touches as bends in the line chart, and it is obvious that the market has respected this zone.

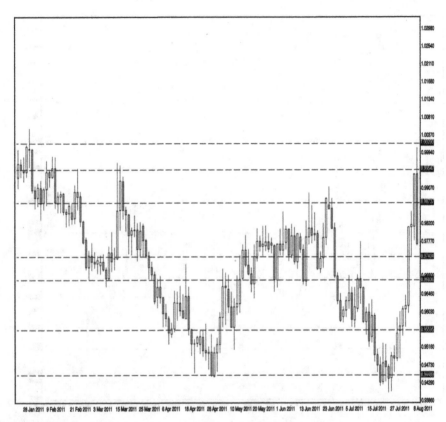

FIGURE 4.24 This is the USD/CAD daily chart again, with only the major zones identified. Notice how the market does not touch a zone every day.
© 2000–2011, MetaQuotes Software Corp.

The fifth problem that you may come up against when trading with zones is this: If the market trades beyond the zone it does not mean that the market has broken the zone. This is an important and critical point for the naked trader. Remember zones are beer bellies, they are squishy, they are fat, and they consist of a wide range on the chart. This means that sometimes the market will push into the zone, and it may look like the market has broken beyond the zone, this is often not the case. Take a look at the daily NZD/CHF chart in Figure 4.28, the market finds resistance at the 0.7590 zone at least five times between November 2009 and March 2010.

The NZD/CHF chart from November 2009 to March 2010 shows a clearly defined zone at 0.7590, the market finds resistance at this level on

FIGURE 4.25 The daily CHF/JPY chart has a clear zone at 89.35; the market has found resistance at or near this zone on several occasions. Notice how some of the valid zone touches are a deep into the zone and others are near the zone.
© 2000–2011, MetaQuotes Software Corp.

at least five occasions. From left to right, there are at least five touches on the 0.7590 zone. The first touch is a near miss; the price came very close to 0.7590, but ultimately found resistance just below this price. The remaining touches are a bit beyond the zone, but each are valid touches on the zone. The second touch includes three daily candlesticks in succession; each day the market pushes a bit beyond the 0.7590 zone. Ultimately, the market closes below the zone, and after the third daily candlestick falls, the market trades lower once again. The third touch occurs five days later and includes a piercing kangaroo tail candlestick (see chapter 8 for more on the kangaroo tail), clearly the market has traded beyond the 0.7590 zone, but the market is unable to close above the zone, and it falls down after this touch. The fourth touch is made up of two candlesticks, the first on the

FIGURE 4.26 The one-hour AUD/JPY chart has several clean reversals around the 81.83 zone; however, there are several sloppy touches marked with arrows. The market does not appear to respect the zone during these touches.
© 2000–2011, MetaQuotes Software Corp.

0.7590 zone and the second pushes a bit further beyond the zone, but it is still a valid touch. (There is another near miss after this touch, not marked on Figure 4.28, but the market does come very close to the 0.7590 zone.) The fifth and final touch again penetrates the zone before falling sharply; notice how the market was once again unable to *close* on the other side of the zone. At times, the market may touch a zone and then close briefly beyond the zone before moving back, but most of the time if the market touches a zone, it may trade beyond the zone, but it will not close beyond the zone.

Have a look at some charts. You will notice how price will often push into and beyond a zone, only to eventually turn around. This is a common

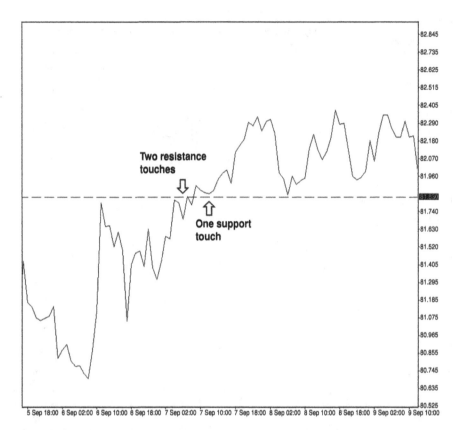

FIGURE 4.27 The line chart clears up the confusing price action around the 81.83 area on the AUD/JPY one-hour chart. The line chart indicates that the market found resistance twice and support once on the 81.83 zone, so it is a well-placed zone. © 2000–2011, MetaQuotes Software Corp.

behavior. It is also the reason why most naked traders find it much easier to trade *reversal* set-ups than breakouts. Reversal set-ups are based on the market turning around at a zone, and breakouts are based on the market trading *beyond* a zone. Perhaps you are similar to most traders in that you find it a very tricky proposition to determine when the market has made a breakout and traded beyond a zone. If this describes your experience, you may consider avoiding breakout trades and focusing on reversal trades. The easiest and safest way to trade breakouts is covered in Chapter 5, The Last-Kiss. If you are interested in breakout trading, the last kiss may be the trade for you.

Once you begin to closely attend to the clues in the market, your trading will become more consistent. Once the market reaches a zone,

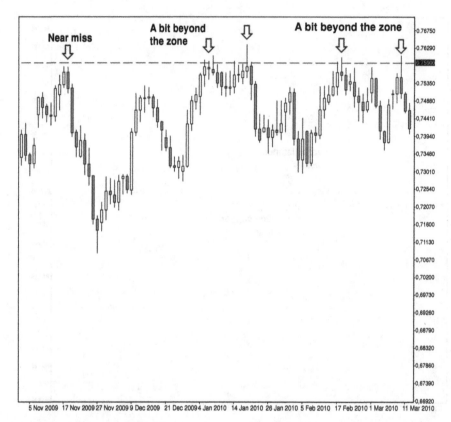

FIGURE 4.28 The NZD/CHF daily chart shows at least five touches on the 0.7590 zone; some touches go beyond the zone, others are just below the zone.
© 2000–2011, MetaQuotes Software Corp.

the naked trader watches carefully, and if a catalyst appears, a trade is triggered. The key to successful trading is to wait for the very best trading opportunities. These opportunities occur when the market reaches a well-defined zone and then prints a catalyst. These are golden opportunities. The next section is all about trading catalysts, how to identify them and specific rules for trading each of the high probability, naked-trading set-ups.

PART TWO

Naked-Trading Methodology

CHAPTER 5

The Last Kiss

*To me, there is no greater act of courage than being
the one who kisses first.*

—Janeane Garofalo

A ll of the naked-trading strategies in this book have three parts: The first is to identify the support and resistance zones, the second is to wait for the market to reach one of these zones, and the third is to take a trade once a catalyst prints on one of these zones.

You now understand how to find zones on the chart, and you are ready to learn about catalysts. Catalysts are powerful price patterns. These simple price patterns suggest what the market may do *once the market reaches a zone*. These catalysts are only useful when they print on a zone; catalysts that are not located on a zone are simply interesting price formations—they are not high-probability trade set-ups. A very simple and extremely powerful catalyst is the last-kiss trade.

If you have been trading for some time, you have probably seen enough of the markets to know that there are two basic moods of the market, and these moods will be seen in any market in the world. There is the calm, drifting, directionless, choppy market as is evident in Figure 5.1. At times, the market will also exhibit strong, powerful explosions characteristic of the trending market as can be seen in Figure 5.2. The market is always in one of these two moods.

Continually, the market moves between these two states: the hyperactive trending market and the relaxed, drifting market (see Figure 5.3). Just as there are low tides and high tides, hot days and cool days, the market

14 Jun 04:00 14 Jun 20:00 15 Jun 12:00 16 Jun 04:00 16 Jun 20:00 17 Jun 12:00 20 Jun 04:00 20 Jun 20:00 21 Jun 12:00 22 Jun 04:00 22 Jun 20:00 23 Jun 12:00 24 Jun 04:00 24 Jun 20:00

FIGURE 5.1 This EUR/USD four-hour chart is in the classic consolidation phase. Notice price movement is choppy, and directionless and does not seem to go anywhere.

© 2000–2011, MetaQuotes Software Corp.

also projects days of laziness (choppy markets) and days of overwhelming activity (trending markets). Traders take advantage of these two moods in the market.

Most trading systems will take advantage of either the choppy market or the strong trending market. This means that most trading systems will perform exceptionally well during either the choppy market *or* a trending market, but never in both types of market moods.

For example, if you decide to trade the trendy kangaroo tail, but instead of waiting for a strong trend, you decide to apply the trendy kangaroo tail to a directionless market, you may find that the trendy kangaroo tail does not offer the type of profit potential you are looking for in a trading system (the trendy kangaroo tail is a naked trading set-up for

FIGURE 5.2 Another EUR/USD four-hour chart, here the market is consistently moving upward in a strong trending phase.
© 2000–2011, MetaQuotes Software Corp.

trending markets, described in detail in Chapter 10). This is simply because the trendy kangaroo tail system is designed to take advantage of a strong trending market. Applying this system to a directionless, choppy market that isn't interested in going anywhere will likely lead to undesirable results. This simple fact means that you must keep in mind which type of market your chosen trading system is designed to work well in, and try to restrict the application of your chosen trading system to only this type of market.

There is, however, one age-old strategy that works on the precipice of the transition from the choppy, directionless market to the strong trending market. This is the breakout strategy. This trading strategy is extremely common; there are many versions of the breakout trade.

FIGURE 5.3 The EUR/USD four-hour chart transitioning between a directionless, drifting mood to a strong trending phase.
© 2000–2011, MetaQuotes Software Corp.

WHAT IS A BREAKOUT TRADE?

The breakout strategy involves two phases. The first phase involves waiting for the market to consolidate. A consolidated market becomes very choppy and directionless, the trader waits, and watches the market. The breakout trader is a patient trader. This strategy is largely based on patience and timing.

Perhaps you have traded a version of the breakout trade in the past. There are many versions of this trading set-up, so you might know the drill: You wait and watch the market when it is calm. You are waiting when the market is trading within a tight range. Then, eventually the market breaks out and extends beyond the restricted range and rockets off in one direction for a strong, sustained trending move. This is where the well-placed entry will capture a quick profit at the very least, and may even afford an early entry into a strong, sustained trend.

Identifying the Transition

As a breakout trader you take advantage of the natural rhythm of the market and, in particular, the transition between the boring, restricted movement of the range-bound market and the fierce strong moves of the trending market. When will you know that the market is changing? How do you determine that the consolidation period is over? Will the market offer a clue when it is about to move into a trending phase?

Is it possible to determine when the market ends the directionless phase and begins the strong trending phase? The answer is yes, and you will use your old friend, the support and resistance zone. The support and resistance zone will be the threshold by which you judge the movement of the market once again. This time the support and resistance zone will mark the line in the sand for the naked version of the breakout trade—the last-kiss trade.

The first step of the last-kiss trade is to identify the consolidation zone. One way to visualize a consolidation zone is to draw a box on the chart. This box will contain the choppy movements of the directionless market. This box should encompass the market movement during the choppy, drifting-market phase (see Figure 5.4).

The important thing to remember here is that the box, which contains the market activity, is formed by both a support zone and a resistance zone. This box of market activity should pop out on the chart—it should be obvious that the market is stuck between both of the zones. Typically, there will be several touches on either side of the zones. In Figure 5.5 we see that there are three touches at the top of the box (market found resistance) and two touches at the bottom of the box (market found support).

The consolidation phase inside of the box may continue for some time. However, once the market breaks out toward either the support zone or the resistance zone, the last-kiss trader takes notice. For many breakout traders, the move outside of the consolidation box will trigger a trade. However, the last kiss trade is not triggered at this stage.

A close examination of a typical, standard breakout trade may be in order. The typical breakout strategy will follow a series of events. First, the market consolidates, and a box is drawn around the consolidation. Second, the market pushes beyond either the support zone or the resistance zone to trigger a trade (see Figure 5.6).

This move beyond the zone is the trade signal. In fact, standard breakout traders often place buy stop orders above the resistance zone, and sell

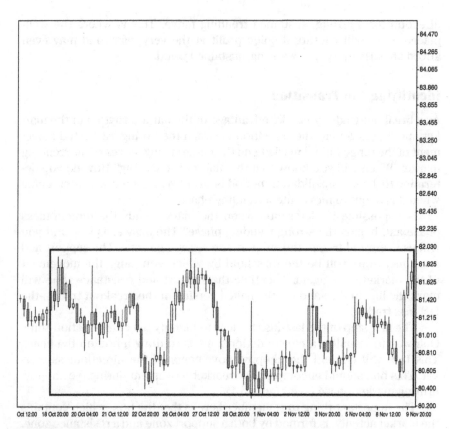

FIGURE 5.4 This box on the USD/JPY four-hour chart may be used to contain the price action in the market during the drifting-market phase.
© 2000–2011, MetaQuotes Software Corp.

stop orders below the support zone in anticipation of the breakout. There are, of course, varying degrees of differences among breakout strategies; however, the core principle that guides breakout strategies is this: Once the market breaks out beyond a zone, a trade is triggered.

However, the standard breakout strategies have a very common problem. Many breakout trades end up as losing trades because they are triggered by a fake-out. What is a fake-out, you ask?

The Fake-Out

The fake-out is the breakout trader's nemesis. This is the biggest problem with most breakout trading strategies. Many breakout signals offer excellent trading opportunities, but others are triggered by fake-outs. A fake-out

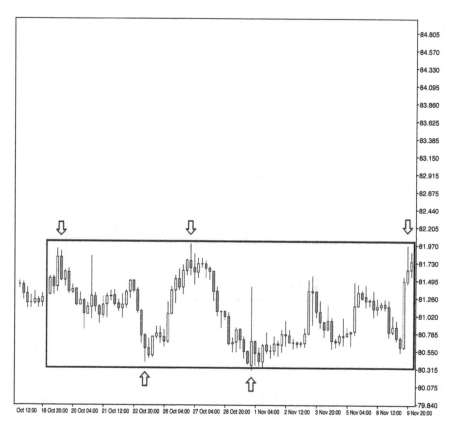

FIGURE 5.5 The consolidation zone should be very obvious. Notice how the market bounces off of the support zone and the resistance zone several times on the four-hour USD/JPY chart. Twice the market finds support at the bottom of the box and three times the market finds resistance at the top of the box.
© 2000–2011, MetaQuotes Software Corp.

is a move outside of the consolidation zone that *appears* to be a breakout, but instead of continuing on in one direction a strong trend, the market retraces *back inside of the consolidation zone.* The fake-out always ends up with the market eventually falling back inside the zone defined by both the support and the resistance levels (back inside the box). The USD/CHF four-hour chart in Figure 5.7 is an example of a fake-out. The strong move outside the box (see arrow) is assumed to be a breakout, but the market retraces and eventually falls back inside the box.

Thus, a fake-out is a breakout trade that is triggered by a convincing candlestick that extends beyond a support or resistance zone. This action is followed by the market moving back inside the consolidation box (see

FIGURE 5.6 This four-hour chart on the USD/CHF shows a standard breakout trade. The trade is triggered once the market moves beyond either the support zone or the resistance zone. In this example, the market breaks out to the upside, signaling a buy trade.

© 2000–2011, MetaQuotes Software Corp.

Figure 5.8). Once the market retreats back into the consolidation box after a fake-out, price will often languish inside the box for some time.

The fake-out is actually quite common, and a quick look at the charts will show how often they do occur.

These failed breakouts, the fake-outs, are the primary reason traders find it difficult to consistently apply breakout trading systems. Breakout systems are simply wrong too often. Breakout systems may occasionally grab a great trend early, but fake-outs signal many losing trades. Why is this the case? Why are fake-outs so common?

Ask any trading guru the question "how often does the market trend?" and, depending on the guru, you will be told that the market trends about 15

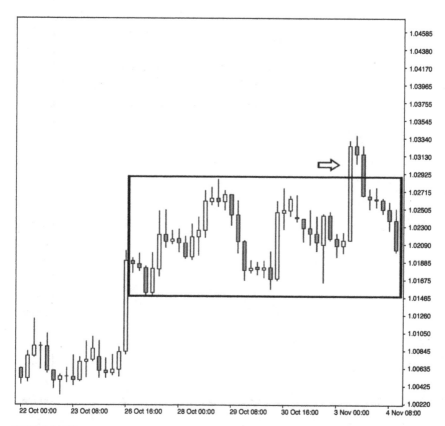

FIGURE 5.7 This fake-out is marked with the arrow on the USD/CHF four-hour chart. The market trades higher than the top of the box, but later quickly falls back inside of the box. For most standard breakout systems this would be a losing trade.
© 2000–2011, MetaQuotes Software Corp.

to 30 percent of the time. *This* is precisely why conventional breakout systems often fail. Most of the time, the markets are not ready to start trending; they spend the majority of the time drifting without direction. This is why breakout trades often fail.

Would it be nice if you could tell when a breakout is going to continue onward beyond the consolidation box? What if there was a way to avoid the dreaded fake-out? Would you like a trading system for identifying the breakouts most likely to continue onward in the direction of the trend? There is such a system, and it is called the last-kiss trade. The last kiss is a specific type of breakout that suggests a breakout will develop into a strong trending move.

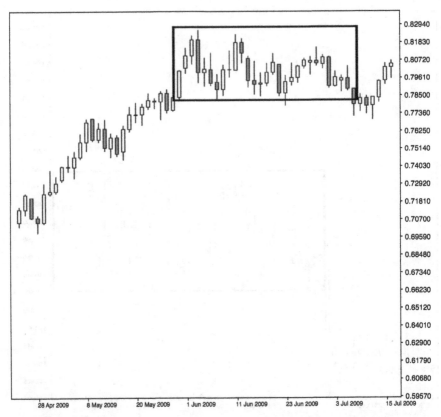

FIGURE 5.8 Another fake-out, this time on the AUD/USD daily chart. The market trades beyond the bottom of the box, triggering a sell trade, but then the market quickly jumps back up inside the consolidation box. This would be a failed breakout trade for most breakout trading systems.
© 2000–2011, MetaQuotes Software Corp.

WHAT IS A LAST KISS?

The last kiss is a catalyst specifically designed to avoid the fake-out. If you have traded breakout systems in the past, you know how often these fake-outs will occur. Although the last kiss is not guaranteed to avoid *all* fake-outs, it will provide you with a valuable method of filtering out many of the very worst fake-outs that fizzle quickly. The last-kiss trade is a simple method that confirms the validity of the breakout signal, and it is based on a sound naked-trading principle. This is known as the retouch principle.

FIGURE 5.9 The consolidation box forms on the EUR/GBP daily chart, followed by a breakout candlestick.
© 2000–2011, MetaQuotes Software Corp.

THE RETOUCH

The market trades beyond a zone before returning to the zone from the other side to confirm the importance of the zone.

A close examination of the last-kiss trade will illustrate how this trade incorporates the retouch principle. Take a look at the chart in Figure 5.9 where a breakout candlestick prints after the market trades between two zones for some time.

The last-kiss trade is not triggered on this initial breakout candlestick but is, instead, triggered much later. The standard breakout trade is initiated when the market moves beyond one of the support and resistance zones. The last-kiss trade is not triggered until later. Why is it important to wait?

Take a look at the losing trades on the previous pages. Do you notice a common theme? The previous charts, the USD/CHF four-hour chart in Figure 5.7 and the AUD/USD daily chart in Figure 5.8 illustrate the problem with many breakout trades. These trades often quickly fizzle as the market moves back inside of the consolidation box. Not only that, but the market often moves back inside the consolidation box *quickly*. This tendency, the tendency for failed breakouts to quickly jump back inside the consolidation box, is the peculiar behavior that is important to the last-kiss trade.

Most of the failed breakouts will quickly jump back inside the consolidation box. However, a true breakout—those trades that extend beyond the consolidation box and then keep travelling—will often move back to

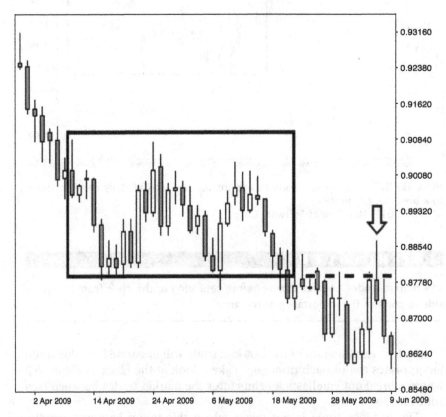

FIGURE 5.10 The last-kiss trade is signaled on the EUR/GBP daily chart once the market returns to the edge of the box for a retouch.
© 2000–2011, MetaQuotes Software Corp.

the support and resistance zones for a retouch. The last-kiss trade is a specific subset of the breakout trade. Not every breakout trade is a last-kiss trade, but every last-kiss trade is a breakout trade.

In other words, the last-kiss trade is based on the retouch principle. The market will often come back to a significant zone once the market has expanded beyond the zone, and the last-kiss trade is designed to take advantage of this typical market behavior (once the market retreats and moves back toward the consolidation box). The reason for waiting for the market to come back to the consolidation box is to confirm that the market will, indeed, respect the boundaries that were formed by the consolidation box. In this way, the trader will jump on the trade only when the market comes back to kiss a consolidation box (see Figure 5.10).

FIGURE 5.11 The EUR/USD daily chart shows two fake-outs preceding the last kiss. The last kiss is triggered once the market breaks out above the consolidation box, and then returns to the edge of the box for a retouch.
© 2000–2011, MetaQuotes Software Corp.

This is why the trade is known as the last kiss. The trade is initiated only when the market returns to the consolidation box to kiss one of the support and resistance zones that formed during the consolidation. This is obviously a very different entry to the standard breakout trading strategy.

The best way to get a sense for the last-kiss trade is to examine a couple of examples. Take a look at the EUR/USD daily chart in Figure 5.11.

Here we see the EUR/USD has had two failed breakouts prior to the last kiss in Figure 5.11. The first fake-out is a false breakout to the upside, but the market quickly falls back inside of the box. There is also a brief fake-out to the downside, but the market drifts back inside of the box soon after that fake-out. The last break out is a true breakout, and it is also a last-kiss set-up. The market trades outside the box to the upside, and then returns to the edge of the box to find support before continuing onward in the direction of the breakout (see Figure 5.12).

FIGURE 5.12 The market continues trending higher after last kiss on the EUR/USD daily chart, notice how the retouch is a nice bullish candlestick.
© 2000–2011, MetaQuotes Software Corp.

Notice how the market prints a very nice bullish candlestick at the edge of the consolidation box in Figure 5.12. It is not enough for the market to simply re-touch the zone and then pause; the market must print a strong candlestick in the direction of the breakout to trigger the last kiss. Big shadows such as the last-kiss candlestick in Figure 5.12 are covered in Chapter 6.

Trading the Retouch

Once the market returns to the edge of the consolidation box, it must print a strong candle in the direction of the breakout. Therefore, if the breakout is a bullish breakout (up), then the retouch candlestick must be a strong bullish candlestick. A buy stop is placed above (see arrow) the high of this bullish candlestick (see Figure 5.13).

FIGURE 5.13 For bullish last-kiss trades, a buy stop is placed above the high of the bullish retouch candlestick.
© 2000–2011, MetaQuotes Software Corp.

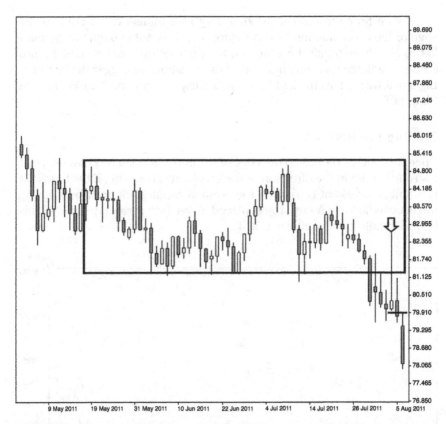

FIGURE 5.14 For the bearish last-kiss trades, such as this one on the daily CAD/JPY, a sell stop is placed below the low of the bearish retouch candlestick.
© 2000–2011, MetaQuotes Software Corp.

Likewise, for the bearish breakouts, when the market comes back to retouch the edge of the consolidation box, the market must print a bearish candlestick. The entry for the last kiss is a sell stop placed below the low (see arrow) of the bearish candlestick, just as you see in Figure 5.14.

Once the market trades through the entry price, the last-kiss trade is on. There are two stop loss signals for the last-kiss trade. The first stop loss is the emergency stop loss, and this is placed at the midpoint of the consolidation box. Under most circumstances this stop loss will not be hit.

The calculation of this emergency stop loss is simple.

1. Subtract the resistance-level zone from the support-level zone.
2. Record the number of pips; this is the width of the consolidation box.

3. Divide the width of the consolidation box by 2.

4. Add this amount to the support-level zone.

This price level is your emergency stop (as shown in Figure 5.15).

The CAD/JPY four-hour last-kiss trade makes for a great example (see Figure 5.16). First, subtract support zone, 85.95, from the resistance zone, 88.23 (85.95-88.23 = 228 pips). Divide this amount by 2 (228 pips ÷ 2 = 114 pips).

Next, add 114 pips to the support zone, 85.95 to find the value for the emergency stop loss. 85.95 + 114 = 87.09, so the emergency stop is placed at 87.09 for the CAD/JPY four-hour last-kiss trade (see Figure 5.17).

FIGURE 5.15 The emergency stop loss for the last-kiss trade is placed at the midpoint of the consolidation box. For this CAD/JPY four-hour last-kiss trade, the stop loss would be at 87.09.
© 2000–2011, MetaQuotes Software Corp.

FIGURE 5.16 Calculating the emergency stop loss for a last-kiss trade on the CAD/JPY four-hour chart.
© 2000–2011, MetaQuotes Software Corp.

There is another exit signal for the last-kiss trade that is more likely to be triggered than the emergency stop loss. If the market closes back inside the box after the last-kiss trade is triggered, the trade is exited. This will usually mean taking a much smaller loss than the emergency stop loss (see Figure 5.18).

This exit signal is usually triggered for a much smaller loss than the emergency stop loss. The GBP/USD weekly chart in Figure 5.18 shows a last-kiss trade that prints this exit signal. The trade is over once a candlestick *closes* back inside the box. Most of the failed last-kiss trades will be exited with this rule. Under most circumstances, it is unlikely that the emergency stop loss at the midpoint of the consolidation box will be hit. The second stop loss is much more likely to be hit, which means that

FIGURE 5.17 The emergency stop loss for the four-hour CAD/JPY last-kiss trade is 87.09.
© 2000–2011, MetaQuotes Software Corp.

the average losing trade for the last-kiss trade is quite small. This is an attractive feature of the last-kiss trade. Many naked traders enjoy trading the last-kiss trade because this second stop loss significantly reduces the size of the losing trades.

Finding Profit after Kisses

One very simple exit for profitable last-kiss trades is to exit the trade at the next zone. There are other, more sophisticated methods for exiting the last-kiss trade covered in Chapter 11.

FIGURE 5.18 This is a last-kiss trade on the GBP/USD weekly chart. The first arrow marks the last-kiss candlestick, where the sell trade is entered. The second arrow marks the candlestick that closed inside the box, triggering the end of the trade.

© 2000–2011, MetaQuotes Software Corp.

TRADING THE LAST KISS

The last-kiss trade is a nice way to trade high-probability breakout trades. Here are the steps for the last-kiss trade:

- Wait for price to consolidate in a box between two zones.
- The box should have at least two touches on both zones.
- Wait for price to break beyond one of the zones.
- Once price returns back to the consolidation box, wait for the market to print a last-kiss candlestick on the edge of the box.

- For sell trades, a sell stop is placed below the low of the last-kiss candlestick, and for buy trades, a buy stop is placed above the high of the last-kiss candlestick.
- Emergency stop loss is placed in the midpoint of the consolidation box.
- The profit target is the nearest zone.

Test the last-kiss trade; you may be surprised at how well this trading system filters out fake-outs. To see live last-kiss trades as they unfold in the market, go to www.fxjake.com/book.

CHAPTER 6

The Big Shadow

Never fear shadows. They simply mean there's a
light shining somewhere nearby.

—Ruth E. Renkel

The big shadow is a two-candlestick, reversal formation and an important catalyst for the naked trader. The big shadow appears on support and resistance zones, precisely where the naked trader looks for high probability trade set-ups. Once the big shadow prints on a zone, we have a valuable hint that the market may soon turn around.

Two candlesticks make up the big shadow formation. As with most naked trading catalysts, they must print on zones to be valid trade set-ups. Big shadows are only valid when they appear on zones. A big shadow may print on top of the zone (the market is finding support on the zone, a bullish big shadow), or the market may print below the zone (the market is finding resistance on the zone, a bearish big shadow). The important thing is this: The big shadow *must* print on a zone.

WHAT DOES IT LOOK LIKE?

Some traders may refer to the big shadow as an engulfing candlestick, but it is more than that, as there are specific rules associated with the big shadow, including how to trade it, and specific optimizers for the trading set-up. The big shadow is essentially a two-candlestick formation in which the second candle completely dwarfs the first candlestick. This second candlestick is known as the big-shadow candlestick. The defining characteristics of the big-shadow candlestick are as follows: The big-shadow candlestick is much larger than the previous candlestick, the big-shadow candlestick has a wide range, and the big-shadow candlestick is the largest candlestick the market has seen for some time.

Figure 6.2 shows another example of the big shadow. This one is another bearish big shadow, this time on the EUR/GBP daily chart.

DOES BIGGER EQUAL BETTER?

If you spend some time watching the charts, you will notice that some shadows are larger than others. The ideal big shadow will have a wide range. Look at the examples in Figure 6.1 and Figure 6.2; both big shadow

FIGURE 6.1 This bearish big shadow on the CAD/JPY daily chart has a much larger range than the previous candlestick.
© 2000–2011, MetaQuotes Software Corp.

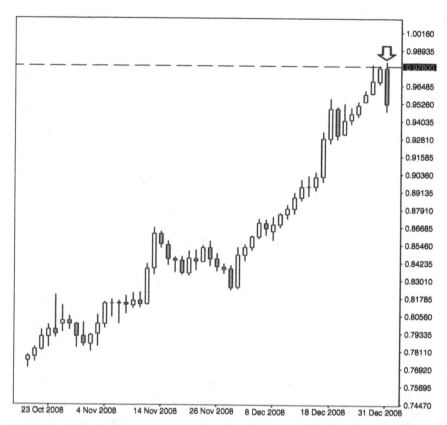

FIGURE 6.2 The bearish big shadow here is on the EUR/GBP daily chart. Notice how the range of the big-shadow candlestick is much larger than the previous candlestick.
© 2000–2011, MetaQuotes Software Corp.

candlesticks have a very wide range. Both of these big shadows are the largest candlestick the market has seen in some time. In Figure 6.1 the bearish big shadow is the largest candlestick the market has seen in several weeks. Likewise, the big bearish big shadow in Figure 6.2 is a very large candlestick, the largest candlestick in over one week of trading.

Ideally, the big shadow should have the greatest range of the previous five candlesticks. Smaller big shadow candles may be tempting because the stop loss is closer to the entry price, but historically, the very large big shadows have a much higher success rate. Back-test this for yourself to see if the very large big shadows you trade have a higher success rate.

FIGURE 6.3 This is a bullish big shadow on the daily GBP/CHF daily chart. The stop loss is placed a few pips above the high of the bearish big-shadow candlestick. © 2000–2011, MetaQuotes Software Corp.

THE STOP LOSS

The big shadow stop loss is placed beyond the big shadow. For a bullish big shadow, the stop loss is placed a few pips below the low of the big shadow candlestick (see Figure 6.3). For the bearish big shadow, the stop loss is placed a few pips above the high of the big-shadow candlestick (see Figure 6.4).

ENTERING THE TRADE

The safest way to enter a big-shadow trade is to wait for the market to push into an expected direction. This will mean using a buy stop for bullish big

FIGURE 6.4 This is a bearish big shadow on the daily GBP/AUD chart. The stop loss is placed a few pips above the high of the bearish big-shadows candlestick.
© 2000–2011, MetaQuotes Software Corp.

shadows, or a sell stop for bearish big shadows. For example, if you would like to enter a sell trade on a bearish big shadow, you may consider placing your sell stop below the low of the big-shadow candlestick. Likewise, for those bullish big shadows, place a buy stop a few pips above the high of the big-shadow candlestick. If the market moves in the expected direction, your buy stop order will be triggered (see Figure 6.5).

Many traders look to enter a trade on retracements, when the market moves against a trading set-up. Although this may seem like a good idea, because it enables an entry at a "cheaper" price, it is also risky. Remember that most traders find it difficult to achieve consistent profits. One of the reasons for this may be because *all* failed trade set-ups will retrace in the opposite direction, but very few failed trade set-ups, such as the big shadow, will take out a new high (for bullish big shadows) or a new low (for bearish big shadows). This is why sell stops and buy stops are

FIGURE 6.5 A buy stop entry is the safest way to enter a bullish big-shadow trade. Here, the market triggers the buy stop of the bullish big shadow on the daily USD/CHF chart.
© 2000–2011, MetaQuotes Software Corp.

recommended for trading the big shadow (and all naked-trading strategies). See Figure 6.6 for an example of how a sell stop avoids a losing trade on a CAD/JPY four-hour bearish big shadow.

It may seem counterintuitive to enter a trade at a poor entry price, but if you decide to use buy stops and sell stops to enter your trades, you will eliminate many losing trades from your record. This is an extremely simple method for avoiding losing trades.

IMPORTANCE OF THE CLOSING PRICE

The closing price is the most important price for the big-shadow candlestick. A big shadow may completely engulf the prior candlestick. A big

FIGURE 6.6 A sell stop entry on the CAD/JPY four-hour chart avoids a losing trade. The market trades higher and never triggers the sell stop entry. Selling this bearish big shadow at a higher price would have resulted in a losing trade.
© 2000–2011, MetaQuotes Software Corp.

shadow may print on a brilliant zone. A big shadow may even be the largest candlestick, with the widest range for a particular market in a very long time. However, if the closing price is not in the correct location for the big-shadow candlestick, the trade may fail miserably.

The ideal closing price for a bullish big shadow candlestick is the high. The big-shadow candlestick has a very good chance of success if the candlestick closes on the high. Obviously, it is rare for the closing price of a bullish big-shadow candlestick to be equal to the high. *The closer the closing price is to the high for the bullish big-shadow candlestick, the better the trade signal.* Bullish big shadows with closing prices near the midpoint of the candlestick are very poor trading set-ups. The naked trader is only interested in high-probability trade set-ups, so if the bullish big shadow

FIGURE 6.7 This bullish candlestick on the daily USD/JPY chart has a closing price down near the midpoint of the candlestick. This is not a bullish big-shadow candlestick formation. Notice how this trade is a loser; the market trades below the stop loss.

© 2000–2011, MetaQuotes Software Corp.

has a closing price down near the midpoint of the candlestick, the trade set-up is probably not good enough to take (see Figure 6.7).

Figure 6.7 is an interesting bullish candlestick, but it is not a bullish big shadow because the market never trades *higher than the high* of the candlestick. Recall that one of the rules of the big shadow is that the market must trade higher than the high to trigger the buy stop which is placed a few pips above the high. Applying this entry rule would have meant avoiding this losing trade. Therefore, the trade in Figure 6.7 has two faults: The market fails to trade higher than the high of the bullish big-shadow candlestick, and closing price of the bullish big-shadow candlestick is too low.

FIGURE 6.8 This bearish candlestick on the AUD/NZD daily chart is not an ideal bearish big shadow because the closing price is not near the low of the candlestick. This trade ends up a loser. The market pushes lower than the low of the big shadow to trigger the trade, but three candlesticks later the market takes out the stop loss. © 2000–2011, MetaQuotes Software Corp.

For bearish big shadow set-ups, the closing price of the bearish big shadow candlestick is also important. The ideal bearish big shadow will have a closing price down near the low of the bearish big-shadow candlestick. A bearish big-shadow candlestick with a closing price near the midpoint is a subpar set-up and should be disregarded (see Figure 6.8). The very best bearish big-shadow set-ups will have a closing price down near the low of the candlestick.

ROOM TO THE LEFT

Would you like to find the trade that captures a critical turning point in the market? You're probably like most traders: You would like to make a trade that catches the market just as it starts to turn around and never returns to the turning point.

If you study these critical turning points in the market, you will notice one thing: All these turning points have a similar look. The price action at these turning points is, generally speaking, extending beyond where the market has been trading prior to the turning point. These turning points are typically exhaustion turning points, that is, places where the market has just gone too far.

There is a far simpler way of characterizing these turning points in the market. These turning points come in two flavors: all-time highs, where the market trades at a very high price, before falling, and never returning to that high, and all-time lows, places where the market falls much lower than most market participants had anticipated, and then rocket higher, never to return to the depths of that low. Traders around the world stare at these spots on the chart, wishing that they had entered a trade at these precise prices, to capture a windfall profit.

There is something that all these turning points have in common. These critical prices are usually stabbed by the market—an exploratory stab, a probe into no man's land. Look to the left of these turning points, and you will find a common theme. Nearly all these all-time lows and all-time highs have one thing in common: There is no price action to the left. Go ahead and take a look right now. Pull up your chart and see if you can find any price action to the left of the very critical all-time highs and all-time lows. Obviously, by definition you will not find a lower price than an all-time low, and neither will you find a higher price than an all-time high. What you will find is that the price patterns are all alone. To the left of these patterns is wide-open space. Have you noticed this on your charts?

You do not have to look to all-time highs and all-time lows; you can simply look to critical turning points—places where the market does not return to for years. The spots will also have this characteristic: The market does not return to those places on the chart where the market rarely trades. So, if we look to take our reversal set-ups at those spots on the chart where the market has not traded in some time, we are putting the odds in our favor.

The easiest way to conceptualize this idea is to look to the left of your price pattern. If you see wide-open space on the chart to the left of your catalysts, you may be looking at a critical turning point (see Figure 6.9), a great opportunity for you to participate in a long-lasting, profitable trade. The general rule is this: The more room to the left, the more likely this spot is a long-term high or long-term low.

Sometimes the market will print a big shadow on a zone that has recently seen market activity. For example, in Figure 6.10 we see the GBP/JPY weekly chart prints a bearish big shadow. Because the market has not printed on this zone for seven weeks, there is some space to the left of

FIGURE 6.9 The EUR/USD weekly chart prints a bearish big shadow. The formation has much "room to the left"—the market has not traded at this zone in over 74 weeks. After this big-shadow formation printed, the marked spent over 22 weeks away from this price.

© 2000–2011, MetaQuotes Software Corp.

the bearish big shadow. Although it would be better if the market had not printed on this zone for 20 or 30 candlesticks, the fact that the market has not printed on this zone for seven candlesticks is perfectly reasonable, and thus this trade qualifies as having "room to the left."

When choosing a big-shadow trade, or any other reversal trade, look to the left of the catalyst. If you see open space to the left, then perhaps the set-up will capture a critical turning point in the market.

However, if you look to the left and you see recent price action at the same level, perhaps the market has not reached the exhaustion stage. Figure 6.11 illustrates a bearish big shadow on the GBP/USD four-hour chart with virtually no room to the left. These set-ups are rarely ideal big-shadow trades. Most naked traders will only consider taking a reversal trade if the market has not printed on the zone for at least seven candlesticks. Reversal

FIGURE 6.10 The GBP/JPY weekly chart prints a bearish big shadow with "room to the left." The market has not printed on this zone for seven weeks, giving this big shadow some reasonable "room to the left."
© 2000–2011, MetaQuotes Software Corp.

set ups with room to the left usually have a much higher success rate than those that print in an area on the chart with recent price action.

An easy way to visualize this "room to the left" rule is to draw a rectangle on your chart that captures the area of the chart that is unique to the *two-candlestick big-shadow formation* and extend this rectangle as far as possible to the left.

TWO-CANDLESTICK FORMATION

A price pattern made up of two candlesticks. The definition and validity of the price pattern is dependent upon characteristics of both candlesticks.

FIGURE 6.11 A big shadow such as this one on the GBP/USD four-hour chart has printed on a zone with a lot of recent price action. Perhaps the market has not reached a turning point yet.
© 2000–2011, MetaQuotes Software Corp.

It is important to note that the big-shadow formation is a two-bar formation. This means that any unique space occupied by this catalyst may be occupied by both candlesticks. Contrast this to other catalysts such as the kangaroo tail (Chapter 8) and the big belt (Chapter 9)—these single candlestick formations may independently occupy unique space on the chart. Remember, the further this rectangle extends before running into other candlesticks, the better. The very best big shadows will print at an area on the chart where the market has not recently traded.

Take a look at the one-hour CAD/JPY chart in Figure 6.12. You can see the market has printed the big shadow on an area on the chart that has not seen recent price action in a very long time. The box to the left of the big shadow represents all of the "room to the left" for this trade set-up. The

FIGURE 6.12 Waiting for big shadows with space to the left, such as this bullish big shadow on the CAD/JPY one-hour chart will aid you in picking high-probability reversal trades.
© 2000–2011, MetaQuotes Software Corp.

market moved 200 pips higher after triggering the buy stop on this bullish big shadow.

PROFITING FROM BIG SHADOWS

There are many methods for exiting the big-shadow trade, many of these methods are explored in Chapter 11. A very simple method for exiting the big shadow is to simply place a take-profit target at the nearest zone. For bullish big shadows this would mean placing a profit target a few pips below the nearest resistance zone, and for bearish big shadows that would mean placing a profit target a few pips above the nearest support zone (see Figure 6.13).

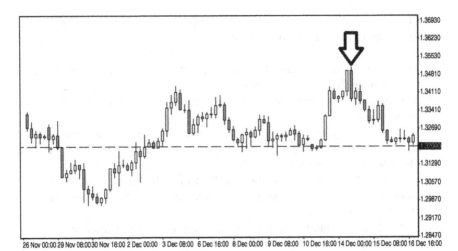

FIGURE 6.13 The nearest zone makes for a very clear profit target. The bearish big shadow on the EUR/USD four-hour chart is an excellent sell signal. The market falls 171 pips down to the next zone at 1.3200.
© 2000–2011, MetaQuotes Software Corp.

THE RULES

The big-shadow trade is easy to identify, and it often signals a critical turning point in the market. Here are the rules associated with the big shadow trade:

- Big shadows are two-candlestick formations.
- The second candlestick of the formation is the big-shadow candlestick.
- The big-shadow candlestick has a higher high and a lower low than the previous candlestick.
- Big shadows must print on the zones.
- Big shadows print at extreme highs or extreme lows.
- Bearish big-shadow candlesticks have a closing price near the low.
- Bullish big-shadow candlesticks have a closing price near the high.
- Big-shadow candlesticks have wider ranges than the nearby candlesticks.
- For bullish big shadows, the stop loss is placed a few pips below the low of the big-shadow candlestick.
- For bearish big shadows, the stop loss is placed a few pips above the high of the big-shadow candlestick.
- The very best big-shadow candlesticks have room to the left.

There are also several optimal characteristics that the best big shadows share; these features include:

- The two-candlestick formation prints at an extreme high or low on the chart where the market has not traded in at least seven candlesticks.
- The big-shadow candlestick has a greater range than the previous 10 candlesticks.
- For bullish big shadows, the candlestick following the bullish big shadow triggers the buy stop order placed above the high of the big-shadow candlestick.
- For bearish big shadows, the candlestick following the bearish big shadow triggers the sell stop order placed below the low of the big-shadow candlestick.
- For bullish big shadows, the closing price for the big-shadow candlestick is within a few pips of the high.
- For bearish big shadows, the closing price for the big-shadow candlestick is within a few pips of the low.

Many traders do extremely well trading only the big-shadow trade. If you would like to become an expert with this trading system, spend time testing it so that you get comfortable trading big shadows. If you would like to follow along with live big-shadow trades, go to www.fxjake.com/book.

CHAPTER 7

Wammies and Moolahs

It's like déjà-vu, all over again.

—Yogi Berra

T he market moves up, the market moves down. If you are a naked trader, you will probably note that the turning points in the market coincide with the support and resistance zones. These turning points are rarely sharp and quick and are, instead, often rather slow to unfold. (There are obvious exceptions such as big shadows, covered in Chapter 6, kangaroo tails, which are examined in Chapter 8, and big belts explained in Chapter 9.) The market usually prefers to hit a zone several times before moving away from that zone. Wammies and moolahs take advantage of this tendency in the markets.

There are five steps to understanding wammies and moolahs. Each of these steps is covered in this chapter. By the end of the chapter you will understand the *theory* behind these two trading set-ups, and you will know precisely how to trade them.

First, the basic double-bottom and basic double-top formations are defined. Second, you will learn the critical characteristics unique to wammies, which are a special case of the double-bottom formation. Third, you will learn all about the moolah, a special case of the double-top formation. Fourth, you will see market examples of both wammies and moolahs so you may clearly understand the idiosyncrasies unique to these formations. Fifth, you will see what an optimal wammie or moolah trade looks like. By the end of this chapter, you will have a clear understanding of both trade set-ups, which are invaluable for the naked trader who is interested in finding important turning points on the charts.

Before you jump into the world of wammies and moolahs, it is important to understand both the double-bottom and the double-top formations.

THE DOUBLE BOTTOM

The double bottom is a classic formation known to many technical analysts. The double bottom is well known because it occurs quite frequently in the markets. Take a look at the chart for any market and you will find many examples of the double bottom; these are places on the chart where the market touches a zone from above and finds significant support after both touches.

DOUBLE BOTTOM

A price pattern characterized by two touches from above on a zone. The market falls to find support on a zone followed by a rally higher and then the market again falls to find support on the same zone. After this second touch of the zone, the market begins a steady climb higher.

Many critical market turnarounds begin as a double bottom. A double bottom occurs when the market moves downward for some time, the market reaches a significant support and resistance zone, the market pauses at this zone and then turns around to begin trading higher. The market eventually stalls and starts to move downward again until reaching the zone once again and finding support on the zone. Once again, the market starts to trade higher and continues trading higher for some time. This is the traditional double bottom.

Take a look at Figure 7.1; this is a typical double-bottom formation. Notice how the market reaches a zone twice and each time it turns around and starts trade higher. It is only after the second touch of the zone that the market starts a new uptrend. This is the defining feature of the double bottom—the market begins a new uptrend after finding support with the second touch of the zone.

This GBP/CHF daily chart in Figure 7.1 is a typical double bottom. After trading lower and lower for some time, the market touches the critical zone at 1.5890 before trading higher for a short period of time, the market once again falls down and finds support on the 1.5890 zone and bounces higher. After the second touch, the market begins a new uptrend.

This double-bottom formation is reliable; under most circumstances, if the market falls down to an important zone and finds support on the zone

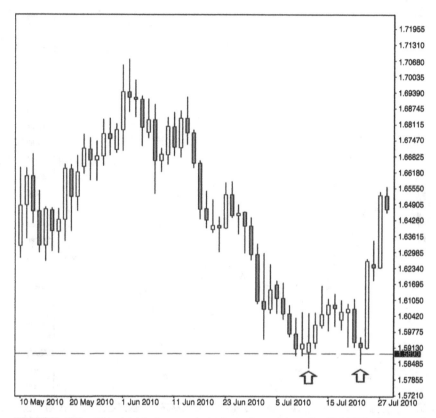

FIGURE 7.1 The double bottom is indicated on this daily GBP/CHF chart by the market touching the zone, trading higher, and then touching the zone again. © 2000–2011, MetaQuotes Software Corp.

twice, it will be likely to trade higher. These double bottom formations are prevalent across markets, much more ubiquitous than the "single bottom." A single bottom is, of course, a single touch (of support) on an important zone. Although the single bottom does occur from time to time (single bottoms sometimes print as bullish big shadows, bullish big belts, and bullish kangaroo tails), the double bottom is much more common in the markets. The market will usually fall down to the zone to test it twice before turning around and marching upward.

Figure 7.2 illustrates another double bottom on the USD/CAD daily chart. Notice how each touch on the 1.5105 zone is distinct. The market falls down, touches the zone, and then briefly trades higher before falling down once again to find support on the very same zone. This is the

FIGURE 7.2 The standard double-bottom formation is created when the market finds support twice in quick succession. The USD/CAD forms a double bottom on the daily chart when the market falls twice to 1.5105 to find support.
© 2000–2011, MetaQuotes Software Corp.

defining characteristic of the double bottom: There is a brief interlude between each touch.

The USD/CAD traded 715 pips higher after the double bottom on the daily chart (see Figure 7.2). This is the kind of move traders dream of capturing. However, not all double bottoms will yield a giant pile of pips such as this one. Some double bottoms end up as losing trades.

In Figure 7.3, the EUR/GBP makes a double bottom at 0.8800 on the daily chart. The market trades higher after the second touch on the zone at 0.8800, a classic double-bottom formation.

Soon after the second touch at 0.8800 zone, the move upwards stalls, and the market falls through the 0.8800 zone, as shown in Figure 7.4. This

FIGURE 7.3 A double-bottom forms on the EUR/GBP daily chart. The market twice bounces off the zone at 0.8800.
© 2000–2011, MetaQuotes Software Corp.

trade would have been a loser for many traders looking to find profits on this classic double-bottom formation.

This is the problem with double bottoms, while many of them identify excellent trading opportunities, some of them are losing trades. Perhaps you have traded this formation in the past and have experienced some winning double bottoms and some losing double bottoms. You may have decided that the double bottom is not a reliable trading formation. If you have dismissed the double bottom, please wait until you learn about the wammie trade, because you may find that there is still hope for the double-bottom trade, or at least for a very *specific type* of the double bottom. Next up is the double top, the mirror image of the double-bottom formation.

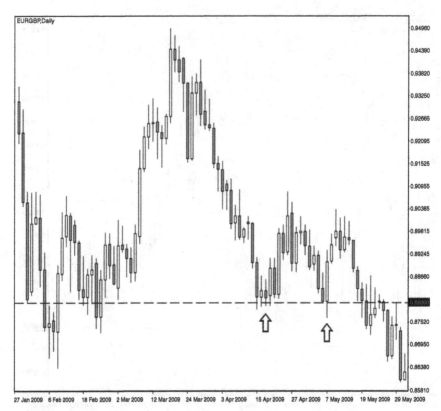

FIGURE 7.4 The market trades as high as the 0.9020 area before falling back down. This classic double bottom on the EUR/GBP daily chart would have ended up as a loser for many traders.
© 2000–2011, MetaQuotes Software Corp.

THE DOUBLE TOP

The double bottom has a sister formation, the double top.

DOUBLE TOP

A price pattern characterized by two touches from below on a zone. The market rises up to find resistance on a zone followed by a fall and then the market again rises to find resistance on the same zone. After this second touch of the zone the market begins a steady move lower.

The standard double top looks like the chart in Figure 7.5: The market trades higher for some time before finding resistance on a zone. The market briefly trades lower before once again rising up and finding resistance on the zone, and then the market begins to trade lower and lower. The defining feature of the double top is that the market begins a new downtrend after the second touch of the zone.

Double bottoms are reversal formations, and they are much more common than other reversals, such as the big belt or kangaroo tail. Markets love to touch zones twice before turning around and moving in the opposite direction. This is why the double top has become well-known in the trading community over the years. It is a classic chart formation.

FIGURE 7.5 The standard double-top formation is created when the market finds resistance twice in quick succession. The USD/CHF forms a double top on the four-hour chart when the market trades up to 0.8500 twice to find resistance.
© 2000–2011, MetaQuotes Software Corp.

The problem with this classic chart formation is this: It often fails. The double top will often print on the charts and then completely fall apart. Some double tops simply do not behave. The double top in Figure 7.6 is a classic example of a double top gone bad. Some double tops simply lose.

Perhaps it is possible to trade a classic double-top formation, even though many double tops end up as losers. Might there be characteristics that winning double tops share? Is there a way to discriminate those double tops which are more likely to fail from those double tops which are more likely to find pips?

The moolah trade is a specific type of double-top formation. A close examination of the definition of the moolah will enable the naked trader to

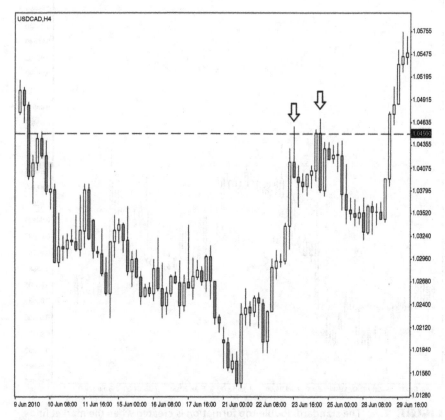

FIGURE 7.6 The USD/CAD four-hour chart prints a classic double-top formation. The market does fall after the second touch at the 1.0450 zone, but soon after the market trades higher and higher.

© 2000–2011, MetaQuotes Software Corp.

decide whether this specific type of double-top formation may improve on the success rate of the classic double-top trade.

IDENTIFYING WAMMIES AND MOOLAHS

Wammies and moolahs occur on any timeframe, in any market, so these catalysts are similar to most of the other naked trading patterns in this book. Wammies and moolahs are unique versions of the double bottom and double-top formations, respectively. You will learn how to filter out subpar double-bottom and double-top trades. Concentrating on only those double bottoms and double tops with optimal trade characteristics (such as wammies and moolahs) will allow you to trade only those double bottom and double tops that offer the high probability of a payoff.

Wammies and moolahs also fit into the general category of reversal patterns. Naked traders who enjoy entering trades at turning points in the market will find wammies and moolahs particularly interesting and useful. Before we jump into these price patterns, it may be useful to list several important market truths. We will incorporate these seven market truths when we look at trading wammies and moolahs.

1. If the market touches a zone twice in succession, it will often move away from the zone.
2. Two touches on a zone from above suggests a market bottom.
3. When the market makes higher lows, it will often continue upward.
4. Two touches on a zone from below suggests a market top.
5. When the market makes lower highs, it will often continue downward.
6. A bullish candlestick on a support zone suggests the market will trade higher.
7. A bearish candlestick on a resistance zone suggests the market will trade lower.

Wammies and moolahs are based on these market observations. If you agree with these market observations, then you may enjoy trading wammies and moolahs.

HOW TO TRADE WAMMIES

As a naked trader, you get paid to observe market patterns, test these patterns to validate their usefulness, and then execute trades based on these patterns. These naked trading patterns occur over and over again, in many markets, on many timeframes. Wammies are a specific subset of the double-bottom formation.

Just like the standard double bottom, the wammie formation includes two touches on the zone, suggesting that the market finds support on the zone. The market will drift higher between the first touch on the zone and the second touch on the zone. The wammie differs from the standard double bottom because the depth of the touches on the zone is critical. A wammie formation is identified by a second touch that is *higher* than the first touch on the zone. In other words, a wammie is defined by a higher low. Recall that a higher low is one way to determine if the market is in an uptrend, this was one of the seven market truths. This subtle difference between a wammie and a standard double bottom may seem insignificant, but this is a critical characteristic of the market's turning points.

In Figure 7.7 we see an example of a wammie trade. The AUD/USD four-hour chart prints two touches in the 1.0560 zone. The second touch on the zone is higher than the first by 34 pips.

FIGURE 7.7 The AUD/USD four-hour chart prints a wammie in the 1.0560 zone. Notice the second touch is higher than the first. The market traded 456 pips higher after this second touch.
© 2000–2011, MetaQuotes Software Corp.

The entry strategy for the wammie is as follows: Once the market prints a strong bullish candlestick on the second touch, a buy stop is placed above the high of this candlestick. Using a buy stop ensures that the trade will only be triggered if the market trades higher than the bullish candlestick. In Figure 7.8, the market prints a bullish candlestick on the second touch of the 1.0560 zone. The buy stop is placed a few pips above the high of the bullish candlestick. Once the market trades higher than the bullish candlestick, the trade is triggered.

The stop loss for the wammie trade is placed below the low of the *first* touch (see Figure 7.9). Placing the stop loss here ensures that if the market is beginning a new uptrend, the stop loss will not be triggered. If the market is moving higher it will not take out the lowest low of the wammie formation.

FIGURE 7.8 The AUD/USD four-hour wammie trade is triggered once the market trades higher than the bullish candlestick on the second touch.
© 2000–2011, MetaQuotes Software Corp.

FIGURE 7.9 The stop loss for the wammie trade is a few pips below the *first* touch on the zone. If the market begins a new uptrend, the stop loss will not be hit. © 2000–2011, MetaQuotes Software Corp.

Wammie trades are designed to capture strong trends. There are several clues provided by the market when a wammie trade prints. First, the market has twice found support on a critical zone. Second, the market has made a *higher* low. This is a critical characteristic of the wammie, because it suggests the downside momentum may be dying out. Third, the market has printed a strong bullish candlestick on the zone *and the market has traded higher than this bullish candlestick,* a strong hint that the market may be ready to trade higher. Taken individually, each wammie characteristic is indicative of a market likely to trade higher, but collectively these characteristics suggest a market ready to take off.

Take a look at Figure 7.10. This is another wammie trade on the GBP/USD daily chart. The important features of this trade are marked with

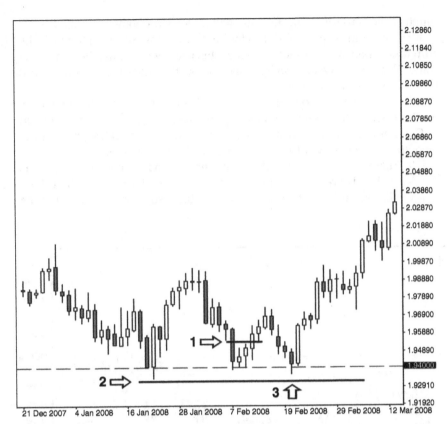

FIGURE 7.10 The GBP/USD daily chart prints a wammie trade set-up. 1. The buy stop is placed a few pips above the first bullish candlestick after the second touch. 2. The stop loss is placed a few pips below the first touch. 3. The market unexpectedly falls back down and touches the zone again, but the stop loss is not triggered and the market soon accelerates 716 pips higher.
© 2000–2011, MetaQuotes Software Corp.

the numbers 1, 2, and 3. At 1, the buy stop is placed a few pips above the first bullish candlestick after the second touch on the 1.9400 zone. Notice that the previous candlestick is *not* a bullish candlestick, because this candlestick closed near the midpoint. This is why the buy stop is placed above the next candlestick, the first candlestick with a close near the high of the candlestick. At 2, the stop loss is placed a few pips below the first touch on the 1.9400 zone. Placing the stop loss here improves the chances that the trade may survive another touch of the zone. At 3, the market falls back down and touches the zone once again. Notice here how the trade survives this third touch on the zone because the stop loss is placed below the first touch. This third touch on the zone will occur after some wammie trades, so it is important to place the stop loss below the lowest (first) touch. If the stop loss is beneath the second touch, this trade would have been a losing trade. With the correct stop-loss placement, the trade survives this third touch and collects 716 pips.

The simplest way to profit from the wammie trade is to simply place a profit target at the nearest zone. More complex exit strategies are covered in Chapter 11, but for now it is important to note that taking profit at the next zone is a great way to manage exits with the wammie.

In Figure 7.11 we see another wammie on a daily chart, this time it is the AUD/JPY. There are five important trade characteristics, each of them marked in Figure 7.11. At 1 the market first finds support on the 75.00 zone

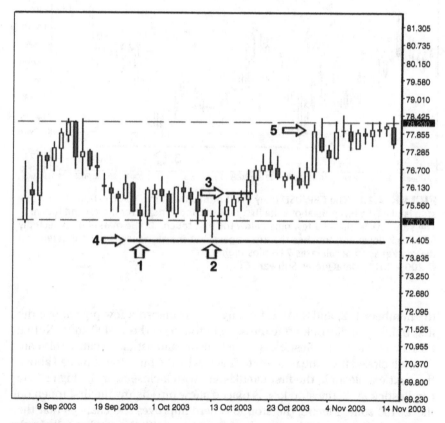

FIGURE 7.11 The AUD/JPY wammie trade on the daily chart has all of the typical wammie trade characteristics.
© 2000-2011, MetaQuotes Software Corp.

with a nice bullish candlestick; the close of the candlestick is up near the high. At 2, the second touch is a few pips higher than the first touch, which qualifies this double bottom as a wammie. At 3, the buy stop is placed a few pips above the second bullish candlestick after the second touch. Notice that there are several candlesticks after the second touch, but the buy stop is placed above the first bullish candlestick with a closing price near the high of the candlestick. Only the second bullish candlestick after the second touch qualifies as a valid wammie entry candlestick. The wammie buy stop should be placed a few pips above the first strong bullish candlestick. At 4, the stop loss is placed a few pips below the first touch for a total risk of 150 pips. At 5, the market achieves the profit target at the next zone at 78.20 for a total of 235 pips.

One final note about the wammie trade: It is important to only take those wammie trades that touch the zone once, move away from the zone, and then touch the zone again. Moving away from the zone after the first touch is critical, and this is why there is a rule for the number of candlesticks between the two touches. A wammie trade is only valid if there are at least six candlesticks between the first and second touches. If there are fewer than six candlesticks, it is likely that the market may be gearing up for a push *beyond* the zone. This is because breakouts often occur when the market repeatedly touches the zone in quick succession. Take a look at the charts, you will probably notice that many breakouts occur after the market repeatedly touches a zone (see Figure 7.12 for an excellent example of this).

The very best wammies will not have very quick touches on the zone, but rather the market will touch the zone, start to trade higher for some time, and then fall back down to touch the zone again. Be wary of wammies with quick touches on the zone, as this may suggest the market is going to push through the zone in the immediate future.

The wammie trade is a simple but powerful trade. Now go back and take a look at the charts in the double bottom section of this chapter. Do you notice anything about the two double-bottom trades? Compare the double bottom in Figures 7.1 and 7.2 to the double bottom in Figures 7.3 and 7.4. What do you notice about those trades? For more on these set-ups and other live wammie trades, go to www.fxjake.com/book.

Wammie Characteristics

These are the seven important characteristics of the wammie pattern.

1. The market touches the support zone twice.
2. The second touch is higher than the first touch.
3. There are at least six candlesticks between touches.

FIGURE 7.12 There are multiple touches on the 0.9400 zone on the USD/CHF four-hour chart. This is a hint that the market is likely to push through the zone.
© 2000–2011, MetaQuotes Software Corp.

4. The market prints a bullish candlestick on the second touch.
5. The trade is entered with a buy stop a few pips above the bullish candlestick.
6. The stop loss is placed a few pips below the first (lower) touch.
7. The profit target is the next zone above the wammie.

HOW TO TRADE MOOLAHS

Now you understand the wammie trade, it will be very easy for you to understand how to apply the same principles to the moolah strategy. The moolah is simply the wammie trade but in reverse. So, where the wammie is a special case of the double bottom, the moolah is a special case of the double top. Like the wammie, the moolah has several characteristics that are critical to the identification of the moolah set-up. Also, the moolah has specific rules for managing the stop loss and a sell stop entry for this trade.

The moolah is simply a double top on an important support-and-resistance zone. See Figure 7.13 for an example of the moolah trade on the daily USD/JPY chart. The important aspects of this trade are marked with numbers in Figure 7.13. At 1, the market makes the first touch on the 119.75 zone and then soon falls lower. This is also where the stop loss is placed, a few pips beyond the first touch at 1 on the chart. The market trades lower, then makes another run higher and touches the 119.75 zone, this time lower than the first touch, at the spot marked 2 in Figure 7.13.

FIGURE 7.13 Moolah trade on the USD/JPY daily chart. The important characteristics of this trade are marked with numbers 1 through 4.
© 2000–2011, MetaQuotes Software Corp.

Notice that there are more than six candlesticks between the candlestick that first touches the zone and the candlestick that touches the zone again at 2 on the chart. At 3, the sell stop is placed a few pips below the low of the first bearish candlestick after the second touch. The market triggers this sell stop on the next candlestick and falls to the first zone at 118.15, but because this zone is only 67 pips lower than the entry price (and the stop loss is 108 pips from the entry price), the trade is held all the way down to the next zone at 117.50, at 4 on the chart, for an overall profit of 133 pips.

The moolah trade is a simple but powerful trade, the rules are simply the same as for the wammie trade, but reversed for double tops. Take a look at the charts in the double top section of this chapter. Do you notice anything about the two double-top set-ups? Compare the double top in Figures 7.5 and 7.6. What do you notice about those trade set-ups? For a video about these specific trade set-ups and live moolah trades, go to www.fxjake.com/book.

Moolah Characteristics

These are the seven important characteristics of the moolah pattern.

1. The market touches the resistance zone twice.
2. The second touch is lower than the first touch.
3. There are at least six candlesticks between touches.
4. The market prints a bearish candlestick after the second touch.
5. The trade is entered with a sell stop a few pips below the bearish candlestick.
6. The stop loss is placed a few pips above the first (higher) touch.
7. The profit target is the next zone below the moolah.

TIPS FOR WAMMIES AND MOOLAHS

It may be tempting to take every wammie and moolah that appears on your charts, but it is important to note that some wammies and moolahs are better than others. If you want to pick only the very best wammies and moolahs, try to do the following:

- Choose the set-ups with many candlesticks between touches. Six candlesticks between touches is nice to see, but 20 candlesticks between touches is better.

- Take trades with catalysts on the second touch. If the second touch is a big shadow or a kangaroo tail, the odds are probably strongly in your favor.
- Pick trades that have a second touch *much* further from the zone. Figure 7.13 is a great example of this type of trade. The second touch is a full 22 pips lower than the first touch, suggesting that the market is running out of steam.
- Only choose wammies and moolahs that are in strong, well-defined zones. If the zone is not an important one, then the market may only trade away from the zone briefly before breaking beyond the zone.
- Find set-ups that have very few zones nearby. This will enable you to place a profit target very far from the entry price and maximize profits.
- Trade those wammies and moolahs that have "room to the left." This idea is covered in the kangaroo tail chapter (Chapter 8). Major reversals often occur at places on the chart with very little price action to the left of the trade set-up.

Kangaroo Tails

Whenever you find that you are on the side of the majority, it is time to reform.

—Mark Twain

The kangaroo tail is an extremely powerful catalyst. It is an obvious clue to the naked trader that the market has gone too far. There are many traders around the world who simply trade this one simple yet powerful trading setup.

WHAT IS A KANGAROO TAIL?

A kangaroo tail is a distinct price pattern. It is one candlestick that is easy to spot. Once you become familiar with this catalyst you will see them everywhere and often at reversal points. Kangaroo tails may print buy signals—bullish kangaroo tails—and bearish kangaroo tails, which are sell signals. The kangaroo tail has two parts: the kangaroo body and the kangaroo tail. All kangaroo tails are single-candlestick formations.

SINGLE-CANDLESTICK FORMATION

A price pattern made up of a single candlestick. The definition and validity of the price pattern is dependent on characteristics of the candlestick relative to the surrounding candlesticks.

FIGURE 8.1 This kangaroo tail on the AUD/USD daily chart is an ideal kangaroo tail because the tail is much longer than the body.
© 2000–2011, MetaQuotes Software Corp.

Ideally, the kangaroo tail is much longer than the body of the kangaroo. The best kangaroo tails have very long tails such as the kangaroo tail in Figure 8.1. The long tail suggests that the market has extended too far into a zone and is likely to reverse. There are other characteristics unique to the kangaroo tail, and all kangaroo tails must maintain *all* these characteristics. If you see a price pattern that does not include all these characteristics, it may be a very interesting price pattern, but it will not be a kangaroo tail.

THE OPEN AND CLOSE

All kangaroo tails have an open and close near the extreme end of the candlestick. For bearish kangaroo tails (sell signals), the open and close of

FIGURE 8.2 This is a valid bearish kangaroo tail on the AUD/USD one-hour chart because the open and the close of the kangaroo tail are both in the bottom third of the candlestick.
© 2000–2011, MetaQuotes Software Corp.

the candlestick should be in the bottom third of the candlestick (see Figure 8.2). If the open *or* the close is not in the bottom third of the candle, it is not a kangaroo tail. There is a similar rule for bullish kangaroo tails: These buy signals must have the open and the close in the top third of the candlestick (see Figure 8.3). If the open *or* the close is not in the top third of the candle, it is not a kangaroo tail.

The open and the close of the kangaroo tail should be near the extreme end of the candlestick. The kangaroo tail is a reversal signal, so when we see a long tail on a kangaroo tail, and the open and close of the kangaroo tail are at the extreme opposite end, we know that the market has moved too far. The kangaroo tail is a clue that the market has extended beyond a zone, perhaps a bit too far beyond the zone. Most kangaroo tails will

FIGURE 8.3 This is a valid bullish kangaroo tail on the EUR/GBP weekly chart because the open and the close of the kangaroo tail are both in the top third of the candlestick.
© 2000–2011, MetaQuotes Software Corp.

print after surprising news; for example, kangaroo tails printed in the forex market during the tsunami in Japan in 2011. Kangaroo tails also printed in the forex market during the global financial crisis in 2008. Kangaroo tails do not only print during extremely surprising news. However, they will often appear when the markets get very excited, and this is often due to some extremely unusual events in the world.

KANGAROO TAILS ARE LONG

Most kangaroo tails are longer candles. This means that the kangaroo tail will be a bit longer than the surrounding candlesticks. Longer kangaroo tails have a tiny body and a long tail. Take a look at the kangaroo tail on the USD/CHF monthly chart in Figure 8.4. The long tail is ideal. The best kangaroo tails will have very long tails and very short bodies.

Why is it important for a kangaroo tail to have a long tail? A long tail suggests that the market has gone a bit too far when testing a zone, whereas a short tail may suggest that the market simply brushed up against a zone. Remember, as a naked trader, you want to look for trade opportunities on zones. Zones, as you recall, are those spots on the chart where the market repeatedly reverses. A kangaroo tail is a valuable clue, a particularly valuable clue when it occurs on a zone. The kangaroo tail with a very long tail suggests the market has become extremely excited before reversing sharply. So, a kangaroo tail on a zone is a high-probability reversal candle at a spot on the chart where the market has historically reversed time and time again.

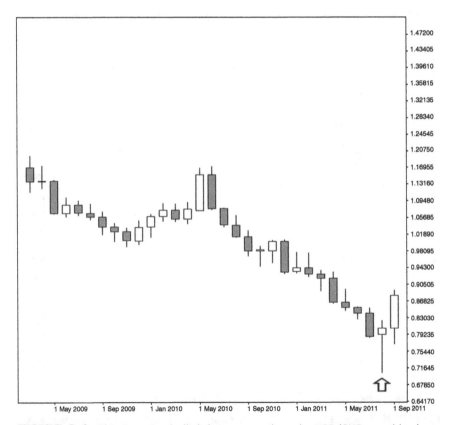

FIGURE 8.4 This is a nice bullish kangaroo tail on the USD/CHF monthly chart with a very small body and a very long tail.
© 2000–2011, MetaQuotes Software Corp.

Here you see how this kangaroo tail penetrated through the zone, suggesting that the market became very excited when pushing price through the zone, and then retreated for the close of the kangaroo tail (Figure 8.5). This is a common kangaroo-tail formation. Most kangaroo tails will push through the zone and then come back and close on the other side of the zone.

The kangaroo tail is a catalyst that suggests the market has gone too far, and has quickly reversed course. Recall that zones are those spots on the chart where the market has reversed repeatedly. Therefore, a kangaroo tail on a zone is a reversal candle on a reversal zone. It is important to remember that as a naked trader you are using price patterns that are clues—hints about where the market may be headed. By trading these price patterns only on those spots on the chart where the market has repeatedly reversed, the odds are in your favor.

FIGURE 8.5 Kangaroo tails often penetrate a zone before closing on the other side of the zone. This bullish kangaroo tail on the GBP/JPY daily chart penetrates the support zone before closing back above the zone at 167.00.
© 2000–2011, MetaQuotes Software Corp.

Kangaroo tails exhibit extreme market behavior. Kangaroo tails often push through a zone briefly (see Figure 8.5) before returning to the other side of the zone.

This is typical of the kangaroo-tail formation, and it is good to see. It is a sign that the market has tested the zone and rejected this level. Exceptionally long-tailed kangaroo tails are wonderful, as they suggest that the market, after pushing through the zone, has gone too far, and then settles back on the zone.

Very small tails on kangaroo tails are not ideal. A small tail suggests that the market may come back and test the zone once again. The USD/CAD daily chart in Figure 8.6 is an excellent example of what often happens after small-tailed kangaroo tail prints.

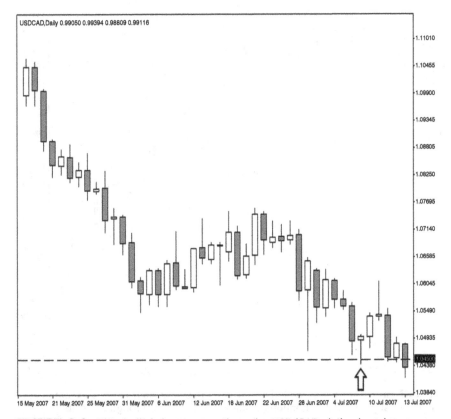

FIGURE 8.6 This bullish kangaroo tail on the USD/CAD daily chart has a very short tail. Notice how the market came back down after the kangaroo tail to test the 1.0450 zone.

© 2000–2011, MetaQuotes Software Corp.

The long-tailed kangaroo tails are often better trade signals than the very small kangaroo tails. The long tails suggest that the market has made a good test of the zone, and then, the zone rejects it. (See Figure 8.7).

When the market prints a long-tailed kangaroo tail, the suggestion is that the market has gone too far. Even though the market went through the support and resistance zone, in the end, the market closed on top of the zone. This is a hint—a very strong hint—that the zone will likely hold the market. A smaller tail on the kangaroo tail does not inspire as much confidence, because a half-hearted test of the zone suggests that the market may decide to come back for a good test of the zone again. Also, during runaway markets, kangaroo tails may print, but smaller kangaroo tails are

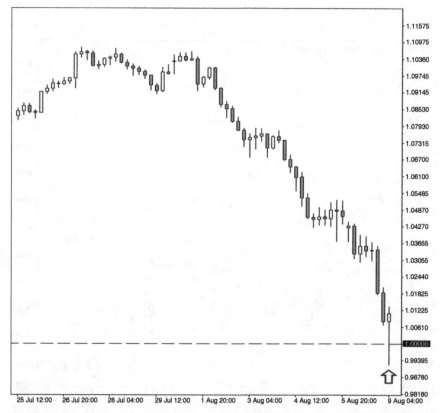

FIGURE 8.7 The kangaroo tail on the AUD/USD four-hour chart is exceptionally long. This suggests that, although the market has pushed through the 1.0000 zone, it has been strongly rejected by the 1.0000 zone. The market moves over 600 pips higher after the kangaroo tail.

© 2000–2011, MetaQuotes Software Corp.

FIGURE 8.8 The GBP/CHF four-hour chart is in a very strong downtrend. Notice the small-tailed kangaroo tail in between the zones. This is not a reliable kangaroo tail trade.
© 2000–2011, MetaQuotes Software Corp.

often simply weak pauses in the market (see Figure 8.8 and Figure 8.9). They often have very small tails and will print in between significant zones; in other words they are not reliable signals.

KANGAROO TAIL PLACEMENT

Kangaroo tails should be near the previous candle. If a kangaroo tail is too far from recent price action, it may suggest a "runaway" market, suggesting the market is not ready to reverse. One way to quantify whether a kangaroo tail is near recent price action is to look at the open and close relative to the nearest candle. If the open and close of the kangaroo tail are inside the

FIGURE 8.9 On the EUR/USD daily chart a bearish kangaroo tail prints in the midst of a strong uptrend. A longer tail on this kangaroo tail would have been a better sell signal.
© 2000–2011, MetaQuotes Software Corp.

range of the previous candlestick, the kangaroo tail is valid (Figures 8.10 and 8.11).

RANGE

The range of a candlestick is the distance in pips between the high and low of the candlestick.

The easiest way to see this rule in action is to look at an example.

The kangaroo tail on the four-hour AUD/NZD chart in Figure 8.10 is an ideal example. Notice the open and the close of the kangaroo tail; both are inside the range of the previous candlestick. It is important for the open and close of the kangaroo tail to be inside the previous candlestick's range

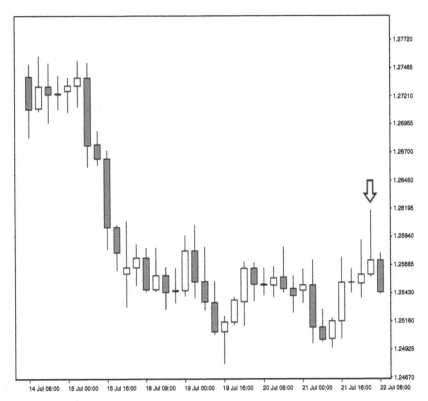

FIGURE 8.10 This AUD/NZD four-hour chart has a bearish kangaroo tail. Notice the open and close of the kangaroo tail are both contained by the range of the previous candlestick.
© 2000–2011, MetaQuotes Software Corp.

because this suggests that the market is not in a runaway trending phase. Sometimes the market will print a kangaroo tail during a very strong trend. When this occurs, you may see the market pause at a zone, but often the market eventually pushes beyond the zone. The four-hour NZD/USD chart in Figure 8.11 shows an example of a runaway market. Notice how the closing price on the kangaroo tail is outside of the previous candlestick's range. This is therefore *not* a valid kangaroo tail. The very best kangaroo tails will have the open and close of the candlestick well inside the range of the previous candlestick. Other candlesticks with an open and close not inside the previous candlestick's range are not valid kangaroo tails.

Look to the Left

Take a look at the chart in Figure 8.12. Notice how in this case the market, the AUD/USD weekly chart, prints a kangaroo tail at an area on the chart

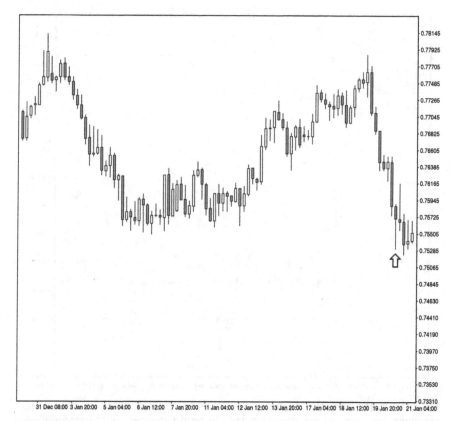

FIGURE 8.11 This candlestick on the NZD/USD four-hour chart is not a valid bullish kangaroo tail. The close of the kangaroo tail is below the range of the previous candlestick.

© 2000–2011, MetaQuotes Software Corp.

that is an extreme high. The market has not traded here in some time, in fact, on the chart we cannot see the last time that the market traded at this level. We could say that this kangaroo tail has much "room to the left."

Why is room to the left important? Why is it that the naked trader seeks out reversal signals that print on the chart on areas that have not seen price action in a long time? The answer is simple: The naked trader is looking to catch extreme reversals, trades that will capture large moves in the market. Ideally, the naked trader will take a trade just as the market is turning around, at places on the chart where the market will not come back for some time. Remember, the naked trader is not held hostage to indicators, so the naked trader has the ability to be nimble and jump into a trade just as the market is turning around, the naked trader does not have to wait

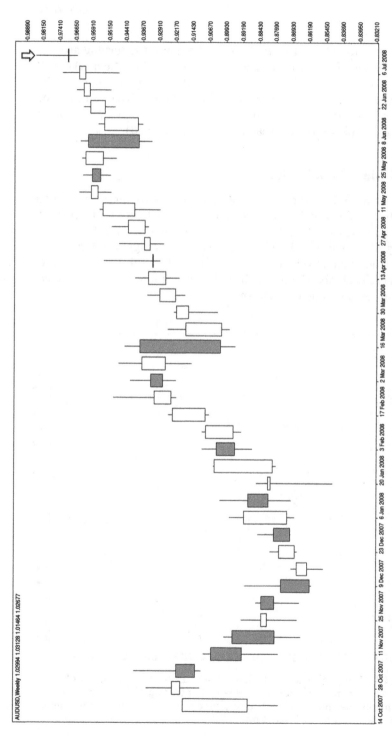

FIGURE 8.12 The AUD/USD weekly chart printed a kangaroo tail at an area on the market chart where we have not seen price action in over 20 years. Thus, we can say that this kangaroo tail has much room to the left. The pair fell over 3,000 pips after this kangaroo tail printed.

© 2000–2011, MetaQuotes Software Corp.

for the indicator to roll over or to indicate the market is turning around. Obviously, the naked trader never knows for certain when the market will make an extreme high or extreme low. The naked trader does, however, know that when the market turns around at an extreme high or an extreme low, at a spot on the chart that has not seen recent price action, the market often does not quickly return to that spot (see Figure 8.13).

Beware of Giant Candlesticks

When the market is in a runaway trend, kangaroo tails often look small compared to the surrounding candlesticks. Take a look at Figure 8.14. This kangaroo tail printed on the EUR/USD daily chart on a brilliant zone. Additionally, the open and the close are inside the range of the previous candlestick, the open and the close are in the bottom third of the candlestick, and there is plenty of room to the left; in fact it has been over 46 days since the market has traded at this zone.

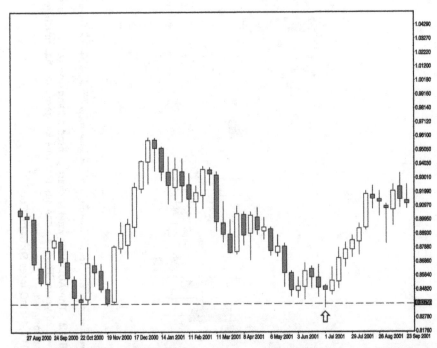

FIGURE 8.13 The weekly EUR/USD chart printed a kangaroo tail in July of 2001. This kangaroo tail has plenty of room to the left, after trading higher than the kangaroo tail, the market has not been back to this zone since this kangaroo tail printed. © 2000–2011, MetaQuotes Software Corp.

FIGURE 8.14 Although this appears to be an ideal kangaroo tail on the EUR/USD daily chart, the giant bullish candlesticks prior to the kangaroo tail hint that the strong uptrend may continue.
© 2000–2011, MetaQuotes Software Corp.

Is this an ideal kangaroo tail? Unfortunately, it is *not* an ideal kangaroo tail. The big bullish candlesticks prior to the kangaroo tail hint that the market may have further upside momentum. Thus, this is not an ideal kangaroo tail simply because the market is printing giant bullish candlesticks immediately prior to the kangaroo tail. Many failed kangaroo tails follow large candlesticks. The best kangaroo tails have a very large range, often greater than the candlesticks immediately prior to the kangaroo tail.

Figure 8.15 illustrates another example of a bullish kangaroo tail. Notice the large bearish candlesticks prior to the kangaroo tail, these candlesticks offer a clue—downside momentum may remain in the market. Optimal kangaroo tails will have a large range, usually greater than the range of those candlesticks immediately prior to the kangaroo tail. Be wary of small-tailed kangaroos.

FIGURE 8.15 This bullish kangaroo tail on the AUD/JPY four-hour chart would have been a losing trade, as hinted by the giant bearish candlesticks prior to the kangaroo tail.
© 2000–2011, MetaQuotes Software Corp.

ENTERING THE TRADE

The obvious entry trigger for the bullish kangaroo tail is a buy stop a few pips above the high of the kangaroo tail. Once the market pushes through the high of the kangaroo tail, it will trigger the buy stop, triggering an entry for the trade. For the bearish kangaroo tails, a similar entry works well: a sell stop a few pips below the low of the kangaroo tail.

Many traders wonder if a different entry technique may lead to greater profits. Specifically, some traders wish to enter the kangaroo tail after the market has retraced or traded in the wrong direction. This may seem like a good idea because the entry may be closer to the stop loss and, therefore, may reduce the risk on the trade. However, the suggested buy stop or sell

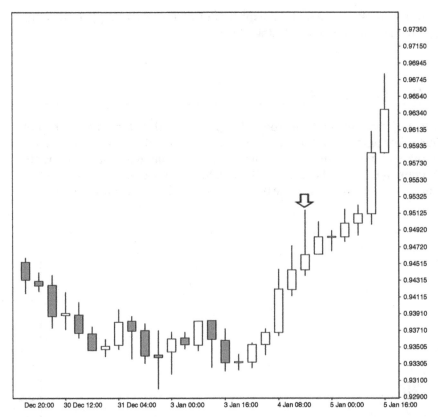

FIGURE 8.16 This is a classic failed bearish kangaroo tail on the USD/CHF four-hour chart. Notice how the market never trades lower than the low of the kangaroo tail. Using a sell stop below the low of this kangaroo tail enables the naked trader to avoid a certain loss.

© 2000–2011, MetaQuotes Software Corp.

stop entry strategy is a much safer strategy because it will avoid many of the losing trades.

Often a failed kangaroo tail will never see the market trade beyond the recommended entry price. For bullish kangaroo tails, if the market keeps falling lower, it may never trade higher than the high of the kangaroo tail (see Figure 8.15). Likewise, for bearish kangaroo tails, if the market keeps trading higher, it will usually never trade lower than the low of the kangaroo tail (see Figure 8.16). Thus, it is much safer to enter kangaroo tails with a buy stop (for bullish kangaroo tails) or a sell stop (for bearish kangaroo tails). Using a buy stop above the high (for bullish kangaroo tails) or a sell stop below the low (for bearish kangaroo tails) will delay the trade entry until the market moves in the expected direction. This simple trade entry technique will avoid many losing trades.

THE STOP LOSS

The stop loss for the kangaroo tail is placed on the other side of the tail, just a few pips beyond the tail (see Figure 8.17). This emergency stop loss is the maximum stop loss for the trade. The emergency stop loss is the maximum loss for a kangaroo tail trade. Ideally, the naked trader will close out a kangaroo tail trade if the trade is in a drawdown and moves 75 percent

FIGURE 8.17 The stop loss is placed a few pips beyond the tail of the kangaroo tail. For this bullish kangaroo tail on the weekly NZD/USD chart, the stop loss is placed a few pips below the low of the bullish kangaroo tail at 0.5480.
© 2000–2011, MetaQuotes Software Corp.

toward the stop loss. Closing the trade before the stop loss is hit will reduce the average losing trade, a very desirable outcome for the naked trader.

PROFIT TARGETS

Chapter 11 covers exit strategies. There are many exit strategies in that chapter that are compatible with the kangaroo tail trade. One simple way of managing the kangaroo tail trade is to take profit at the very next zone (see Figure 8.18).

FIGURE 8.18 A very simple and powerful exit strategy for the kangaroo tail is this: Take profit at the very next zone. After the bullish kangaroo tail on the NZD/USD weekly chart, the market trades higher and eventually finds the 0.6600 zone for a profit of 853 pips.

© 2000–2011, MetaQuotes Software Corp.

KANGAROO-TAIL TIPS

There are several optimizers associated with the kangaroo-tail trade. If you have the patience to wait for only the very best kangaroo tails, watch for the following characteristics:

- Kangaroo tails with a very long tails.
- Kangaroo tails with much room to the left. The ideal kangaroo tails print at an area on the chart that has not seen price action in a long time.
- Bullish kangaroo tails with a closing price that is higher than the opening price.
- Bearish kangaroo tails with a closing price that is lower than the opening price.
- The candlestick after the bullish kangaroo tail trades higher than the high of the kangaroo tail.
- The candlestick after the bearish kangaroo tail trades lower than the low of the kangaroo tail.
- Kangaroo tails with a greater range than the previous 10 candlesticks.
- Kangaroo tails that trigger the buy stop or sell stop entry on the first candlestick after the kangaroo tail.

There are also several red flags, so watch out for these:

- Kangaroo tails with very short tails.
- Kangaroo tails that do not print on a zone; these are not valid kangaroo tails.
- Kangaroo tails preceded by giant candlesticks. This suggests that the trend may continue, and the kangaroo tail may only be a pause.
- When the open and the close of the kangaroo tails are not contained by the range of the previous candlestick.

If you back-test the kangaroo tail, you may find that this trade set-up consistently identifies key turning points in the market. Go to www.fxjake.com/book for live market kangaroo-tail updates.

CHAPTER 9

The Big Belt

It is great to be a blonde. With low expectations it's very easy to surprise people.

—Pamela Anderson

T here are a few moments in life that eclipse all others. Some of them are obvious, and you anticipate them: the birth of your first child, your adventures at an exotic faraway land, meeting someone who will become one of the most important people in your life, and so forth. Other moments seem to come from nowhere, out of the blue, but they are often just as critical and just as important. The first time you realize you will become a profitable as a naked trader may be one such moment. The tricky thing about these surprising moments is this: You never know when they will occur, and when they do, it is important to seize them. These critical, beautiful moments come and go, but you must be ready for them at any time.

WHAT IS A BIG BELT?

This next catalyst, the big belt, is much like a brilliant peak experience in life. A big belt is a very significant occurrence in the market. Big belts rarely occur, and when they do they will nearly always occur on a support and resistance zone. The big belt will nearly always occur on the very first day of the trading week, after the market has had some time to think about a fair price over the weekend.

151

Unfortunately, many traders are a bit too excited when the market starts trading again for a new week. Many traders are thinking about what happened the previous week. Because traders are thinking about the world events *of the previous week*, the market often makes some extreme jumps on the first trading day of the week. Unfortunately, this early excitement is often misplaced, and pushes the market to a place that is a bit too far. When this occurs a big belt will often appear on the chart.

There are two types of big belts: bearish big belts and bullish big belts. Once you understand the basics of the bearish big belt, you can easily apply your knowledge to the bullish big belt, since the trade set-ups are simply opposites.

THE BEARISH BIG BELT

A bearish big belt will occur at a market high and a bullish big belt will occur at market low. In both cases the belts will print on a zone. In Figure 9.1 we see a bearish big belt on the AUD/USD daily chart. The defining characteristic of the bearish big belt is the jump in the market price. In forex, bearish big belts nearly always surface on the first trading day of the week. The market opens much higher than the closing price of the previous week and then steadily trades lower, eventually closing near the low of the candlestick. Thus, the candlestick has a beltlike appearance. The opening price is near the high and the close is near the low. Naturally, bearish belts will also stick out above recent price action. Notice that the bearish big belt prints on the 0.9335 zone. This is a critical zone because the market reversed here after touching the zone four months prior. Bearish big belts will always have an opening price near the high of the candlestick, and the closing price will be near the low of the candlestick.

A bearish big belt has an entry very similar to a bearish kangaroo tail or a bearish big shadow. A sell stop is simply placed just below the low of the bearish big belt. Placing the entry here ensures that the market must make a new low before the trade is triggered. This will, of course, enable you to avoid many losing trades, particularly those signals that follow a rising market. If the market never falls to the entry price, the trade will not be triggered.

Bearish big belts often occur at critical turning points, when the market has become extremely excited. This excitement is translated into a bearish big belt; it is a signal that the market has gone up too far. If you take a look at the bearish big belts on your charts, you will see that, historically, the daily bearish big belts have an exceptionally high win rate. Test this for yourself; scroll through the historical charts and record the market movement after big belts, or test them in a forex tester, or your chosen program

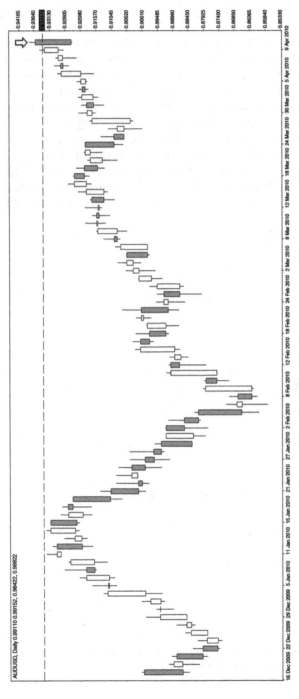

FIGURE 9.1 This is a bearish big belt on the AUD/USD daily chart. The candlestick prints on an important zone, the bearish big belt opens higher than the previous candlestick, open is near the high, and the close is near the low. © 2000–2011, MetaQuotes Software Corp.

for back testing. You may be surprised with the win rate of the big belt trading set-up.

Although it is common to see bearish big belts on lower time frames, such as the one-hour chart and the four-hour chart, sticking to the daily charts only will enable you to maintain a high win rate when trading this set-up. So, although it may be tempting to multiply your trades by taking big belts on a lower timeframe, it is probably a better idea to either stick to the daily charts for this naked trading set-up or be very selective with the trades that you decide to take on the lower timeframes.

As with many of the other naked trading set-ups, an easy way to exit your bearish big belt trade is to simply wait for the market to reach the very next zone (see Figure 9.2). This is often a simple way to capture a large chunk of the move. Again, remember that the bearish big belts often

FIGURE 9.2 Another bearish big belt on the GBP/USD daily chart. A profit target at the next zone captured 385 pips on this trade.
© 2000–2011, MetaQuotes Software Corp.

print at critical market highs, so they offer an excellent opportunity for you to take a bite out of a big move in the market.

The stop loss for the bearish big belt is placed above the high of the belt. If the market trades higher than the high of the bearish big belt, then, obviously, the belt has not identified a key turning point in the market. Take a look at the bearish big belt trade in Figure 9.3.

The bearish big belt is an excellent trade set-up, you simply have to wait for them to occur. If you are watching only the major currency pairs (EUR/USD, USD/CHF, USD/JPY, GBP/USD) you may occasionally luck into a bearish big belt trade. But if you expand your scope, and look at many of the other currency pairs (NZD/JPY, EUR/CAD, GBP/CAD, etc) you obviously have a much better chance of catching one of these bearish big belt set-ups. Back test the bearish big belt on your own to see how profitable and successful these trades may be for you. All you have to do to be ready

FIGURE 9.3 This is the bearish big belt on the GBP/USD daily chart. Notice the sell stop is placed below the low of the belt candlestick and the stop loss is above the high. The profit target at the next zone captured 163 pips on this trade.
© 2000–2011, MetaQuotes Software Corp.

for the daily bearish big belt is to watch the market after the close of the very first trading day of the week.

THE BULLISH BIG BELT

The other big belts are, of course, the bullish variety, bullish big belts are important catalysts that hint at the market moving higher. A bullish big belt will often print at an important market low on a zone. The bullish big-belt candlestick has an opening price much lower than the closing price of the previous candlestick. The bullish big belt will have an opening price down near the low for the candlestick, and the closing price will be up near the high of the candlestick. In Figure 9.4 a bullish big belt is on the EUR/CAD daily chart. This bullish big belt prints on the 1.3430 zone. This is a critical zone because the market reversed here after touching the zone three months prior. The bullish big belts will always have an opening price near the low of the candlestick, and the closing price will be near the high of the candlestick.

The bullish big belt on the EUR/CAD daily chart (Figure 9.4) is an excellent example because the bullish big belt daily candlestick prints on the important zone at 1.3430. The interesting thing about this particular bullish big belt is that the low of the candlestick is a bit lower than the opening price. This is not ideal, but the most important characteristic of the bullish big belt candlestick holds true in this example. The closing price is very near the high price, and this is absolutely critical for the bullish big belt set-up (just as it is critical for the bearish big belt set-up to have a close near the low of the candlestick). Take a look at the chart again in Figure 9.5, here you will see that the stop loss is down below the low of the bullish big belt and the buy stop is placed a few pips above the high of the bullish big belt candlestick, the trade is triggered only once the market trades higher than the bullish big belt. This trade easily achieved the profit target at the very next zone, the 1.3885 area for a profit of 313 pips.

Although the bullish big belt trade is an excellent trade and many traders will find a high win percentage associated with this trade, there are losing trades, just as there are for all trading systems. The next bullish big belt example is in Figure 9.6, this is a weekly USD/CHF chart. Note that the stop loss is placed below the low of the bullish big belt candlestick. The candlestick has good form, the open of the candlestick is down near the low of the candlestick, and the closing price is up near the high. The buy stop entry is placed a few pips above the high of the candlestick, and this entry price is easily triggered during the next candlestick, in fact, the market pushes all the way up to the very next zone.

However, the risk on this trade is 210 pips (from the buy stop to the stop loss), and the first zone is only 180 pips away. Therefore, some traders

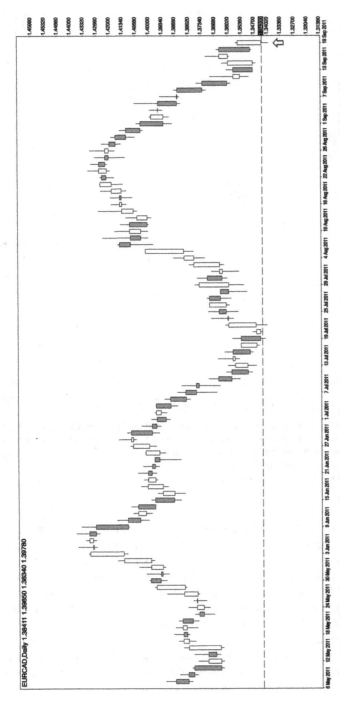

FIGURE 9.4 A bullish big belt on the EUR/CAD daily chart. The candlestick prints in an important zone, the 1.3430 zone. Notice how the bullish big belt opens much lower than the close of the previous candlestick, the open is near the low, and the close is near the high.

© 2000–2011, MetaQuotes Software Corp.

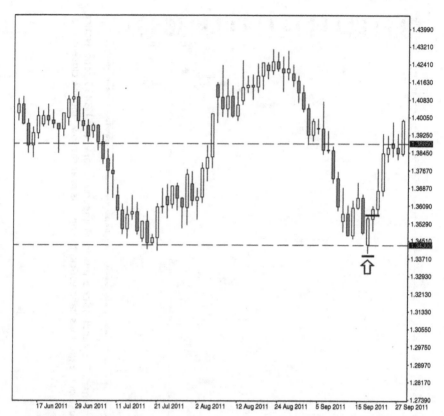

FIGURE 9.5 The entry price for the bullish big belt on the EUR/CAD daily chart is a few pips above the high of the bullish big belt candlestick. The stop loss order trade is below the low of the bullish big-belt candlestick. The profit target is the very next zone at 1.3885, a profit of 313 pips.
© 2000–2011, MetaQuotes Software Corp.

may be more comfortable with a profit target placed at the next zone at 1.2450, a full 425 pips away. This further profit target obviously allows for a much more favorable reward to risk ratio. Exit strategies are covered in Chapter 11, where scenarios such as this one are examined. For now, it is important to note that although the market did go in the expected direction, it only went as high as the very next zone. Your win rate with the bullish big-shadow strategy may depend on how aggressive you are with your profit targets.

Take some time to test the bullish big belt strategy. As with all these catalysts, you may decide to use this strategy along with one of the exit strategies from the exit chapter (Chapter 11).

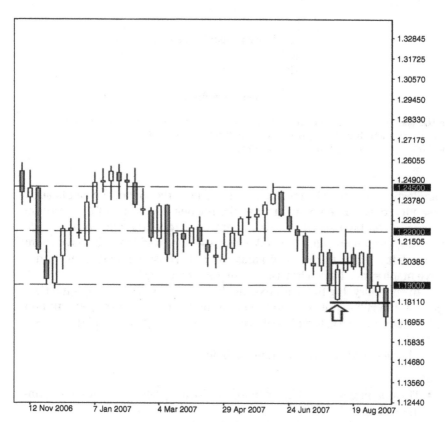

FIGURE 9.6 The weekly USD/CHF bullish belt has a stop loss below the low and the buy stop entry is above the high. The market does reach the next zone, but soon after quickly falls beyond the stop loss price.
© 2000–2011, MetaQuotes Software Corp.

TIPS TO TRADING THE BIG BELT

The rules for the bearish big belt and the bullish big belt are essentially the same, but in reverse. The important things to remember for this catalyst are as follows: All bullish big belt candlesticks have an opening price that is lower than the closing price of the previous candlestick; likewise, all bearish big belts have an opening price that is higher than the closing price of the previous candlestick. The bullish big belt must have an opening price near the low of the candlestick, and it must also have a closing price near the high of the candlestick (see Figure 9.7). The reverse is true for the bearish big belts: The opening price must be near the high of the

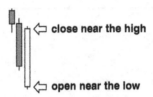

FIGURE 9.7 Bullish big belts must have the opening price near the low of the candlestick and the closing price near the high of the candlestick.
© 2000–2011, MetaQuotes Software Corp.

candlestick, and the closing price must be near the low of the candlestick (see Figure 9.8). Even more critical, the big belt candlestick must print on a zone. If the big belt candlestick is not on a zone, the odds of the trade working out fall considerably. Likewise, the very best big belts have room to the left, similar to the ideal kangaroo tail. Those big belts that do not have much space have a low rate of success (see Figure 9.9).

In summary, big belts are extremely powerful catalysts provided they print at the right spot on your chart. In the list that follows, you will find a summary of characteristics of both the bearish big belts and the bullish big belts.

Characteristics of the bearish big belts:

- The opening price is higher than the closing price of the previous candlestick.
- The opening price is near the candlestick high.
- The closing price is near the candlestick low.
- The big belt prints on an important zone.
- The big belt should have room to the left.
- The stop loss is placed above the candlestick high.
- The sell stop is placed below the candlestick low.
- The closest zone is the profit target.

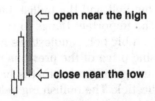

FIGURE 9.8 Bearish big belts must have the opening price near the high of the candlestick and the closing price near the low of the candlestick.
© 2000–2011, MetaQuotes Software Corp.

FIGURE 9.9 Big belts must print on a zone, and they should have room to the left. Those belts that do not print in a zone and do not have room to the left are unlikely to succeed, such as this EUR/USD weekly bullish big belt.
© 2000–2011, MetaQuotes Software Corp.

Characteristics of the bullish big belts:

- The opening price is near the low of the candlestick.
- The closing price is near the high of the candlestick.
- The big belt prints on an important zone.
- The big belt should have room to the left.
- The stop loss is placed below the candlestick low.
- The buy stop is placed above the candlestick high.
- The closest zone is the profit target.

Every week we take a look at big belt trades as they unfold in real time. To join this free online webinar go to www.fxjake.com/book.

CHAPTER 10

The Trendy Kangaroo

Those who try to lead the people can only do so by following the mob.

—Oscar Wilde

A t times the market will take off in a strong trend. These trends make for pretty-looking charts. The market might be marching upward, with very few pauses along the way, or the market could be in a freefall, stopping here and there on the way to lower lows. Any trader who scrolls back through the charts will notice these exciting times and may wish for a method of capturing easy profits from these trending markets. The trendy kangaroo is one such method. This is a way for you, the naked trader, to identify the trend and capture healthy profits from a trending market.

WHAT IS A TRENDY KANGAROO?

The trendy kangaroo is a special case of the kangaroo-tail trade. This is a specific method for jumping on trends. This price pattern does involve a kangaroo tail, but the overall set-up in relation to the nearby candlesticks is very different from the standard kangaroo tail. In fact, the defining feature of the trendy kangaroo is that it must print during a trending market. Obviously it does not matter if the market is trending upward or downward; the key characteristic here is that the market is trending.

It seems nearly every trader has a different definition of a trending market. The large majority of technical indicators are used to identify a trending versus nontrending market. Naturally, as a naked trader, you have no need for indicators, even when you are determining whether any market is trending. To determine whether any market is trending, you will need a consultant.

TREND INDICATORS

You will need several things to identify a trending market. First, you will need some cookies or otherwise tasty treats (maybe some strawberries, some chocolate, or an apple). Second you will need your favorite charts, set to a line chart. Third, and finally, you will need a consultant. This consultant should be between the ages of 6 and 10 years. You may need to call around to find a consultant of the appropriate age, but this is well worth the effort. Friends, neighbors, and distant relatives may be invaluable in aiding you on your search for your consultant. Once you have your consultant, you are ready to determine the trend.

Please do not be tempted to purchase a fancy technical indicator to determine if a market is trending. All you really need is an eight-year-old. All you have to do is point to a line chart and ask your consultant this question: "Is this line going mostly up, mostly down, or mostly up and down?"

Your consultant will tell you all that you need to know. After this brief session you may pay your consultant the agreed-on fee and go forth with your trading. I would encourage you to use this method whenever you are unsure whether the market is trending or in a consolidation phase.

Obviously, you must choose the chart carefully when you do this. If you mostly trade the daily charts, make sure that your consultant has a good look at the daily chart. If you mostly trade the one-hour charts, make sure that your consultant provides an assessment of the one-hour chart. The market is always trending in one timeframe or another, so the question that you present to your consultant should be limited to the market and timeframe you are interested in trading.

If your consultant has identified that the market is trending, you are now ready for the trendy kangaroo tail.

TRADING TRENDY KANGAROOS: RESTING SPOTS

Once your consultant has filed his report, you will know precisely if the market is trending. If your consultant reports that a trend has formed on the charts, it's time to look for trendy kangaroos. Trendy kangaroos are places on the chart where the market has paused to take a rest.

You will know the market is resting when you see several (usually 3–10) candlesticks in a small consolidation zone. This is unlike the consolidation box used for the last-kiss trade, because this consolidation can be something as simple as three small candlesticks that do not seem to go very far. The market is resting after some strong trending moves upward (see Figure 10.1).

If the market is in a strong downtrend, a market pause will look much the same. There will be several candlesticks (again, usually between 3 and 10) all trading within a tight range. This is your clue to get ready because a trendy kangaroo may appear (see Figure 10.2).

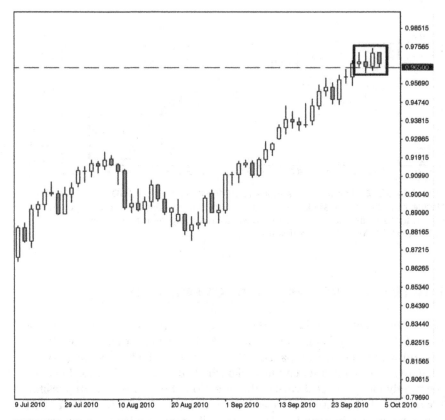

FIGURE 10.1 This is a market pause during an uptrend on the AUD/USD daily chart. Notice how all four candlesticks trade inside the box.
© 2000–2011, MetaQuotes Software Corp.

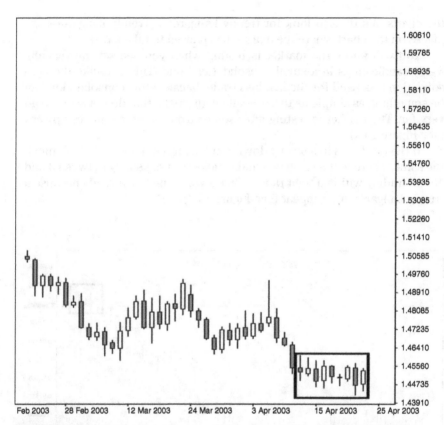

FIGURE 10.2 The market is in a strong downtrend on the USD/CAD daily chart. Notice how the candlesticks are restricted to a tight consolidation range. All the candlesticks trade across the same price range during the market pause.
© 2000–2011, MetaQuotes Software Corp.

TRENDY KANGAROO CHARACTERISTICS

The critical characteristic of the trendy-kangaroo-trading set-up is, of course, the trendy kangaroo candlestick. This candlestick will stick out beyond where the market paused. It is critical for the trendy kangaroo to print away from the other candlesticks which are stuck in the box. Because the trendy kangaroo is always in the direction of the trend, it is impossible for the trendy kangaroo to have a large amount of room to the left. This is in contrast to the standard kangaroo-tail trade. The trendy kangaroo is judged by how far the tail sticks out beyond the recent market pause. If there is much of the tail sticking out in an area on the chart where the recent candlesticks have not traded, then the trendy kangaroo is deemed an excellent trading set-up. In Figure 10.3 we see the AUD/USD daily chart with a trendy kangaroo which sticks out beyond the recent market pause. This is an excellent trendy kangaroo set-up.

The same holds true for a trendy kangaroo that pops up during a down-trend. The trendy kangaroo has a long tail that sticks out above the market pause. The trendy kangaroo will never have much room to the left simply because it prints during a strong trend. However, the trendy kangaroo should always print away from the recent consolidation. The more the candlestick prints away from the market pause the better. Take a look at the chart in Figure 10.4—the USD/CAD daily chart prints an excellent trendy kangaroo during a strong downtrend.

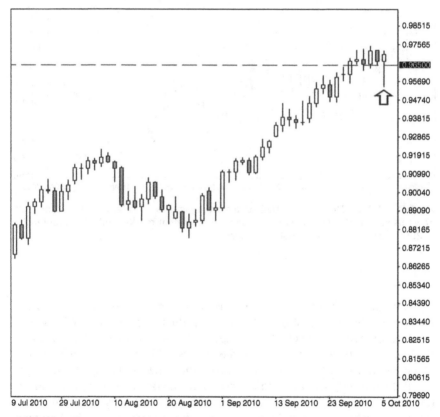

FIGURE 10.3 The trendy kangaroo appears on the AUD/USD daily chart. The trendy kangaroo must stick out beyond the market pause. It is important for the trendy kangaroo to stick out beyond where the recent market pause has traded.
© 2000–2011, MetaQuotes Software Corp.

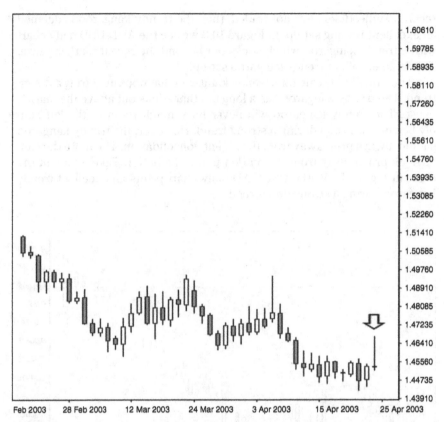

FIGURE 10.4 This daily USD/CAD trendy kangaroo is an excellent example of how this candlestick should stick out beyond the recent market consolidation range. © 2000–2011, MetaQuotes Software Corp.

Bearish trendy kangaroo trades are traded much like standard bearish kangaroo tails. The sell stop is placed below the low of the trendy kangaroo candlestick. Once this sell stop is triggered, the stop loss is placed above the high of the trendy kangaroo candlestick. See Figure 10.5 for an example of a bearish trendy kangaroo-tail trade on the USD/CAD daily chart.

Bullish trendy kangaroo tails are similar to standard bullish kangaroo-tail trades. Once the market prints the trendy kangaroo, you may manage this trade just as you would a normal bullish kangaroo tail trade. You may place the buy stop above the high of the trendy kangaroo. The stop loss goes on the other side of the tail. So for a bullish trendy kangaroo tail, the stop loss is placed below the low (see Figure 10.6).

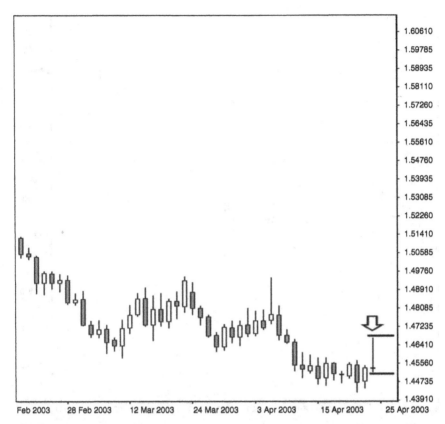

FIGURE 10.5 The trendy kangaroo is managed in much the same way as a standard kangaroo-tail trade. The sell stop is placed below the low of the trendy kangaroo candlestick. The stop loss is placed above the high for this bearish trendy kangaroo on the USD/CAD daily chart. The market fell over 1000 pips after this trendy kangaroo tail printed.
© 2000–2011, MetaQuotes Software Corp.

The trendy kangaroo tail will often print on an important zone. Take a look at the four-hour GBP/CHF chart in Figure 10.6. The market pauses at the 0.96500 zone. Several candlesticks find support on the 0.96500 zone before the bullish trendy kangaroo tail prints. This trendy kangaroo tail offers a clue; the market is ready to start marching higher again. After the trendy kangaroo prints the market moves 317 pips higher over the next two days.

A few more examples of the trendy kangaroo set-up will help you to identify the difference between a good trendy kangaroo and a poor trendy kangaroo. In Figure 10.7, the market prints a nice bullish trendy kangaroo

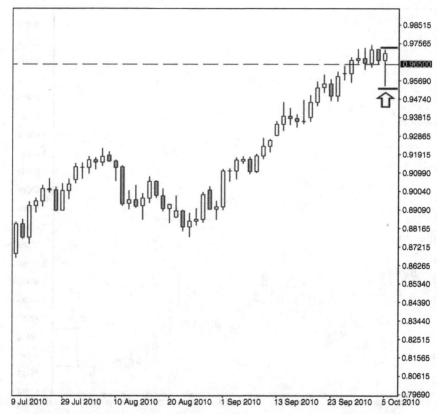

FIGURE 10.6 This bullish trendy kangaroo candlestick on the daily AUD/USD chart suggests the market will soon move higher. Within two days the market moves 175 pips higher than the entry price.
© 2000–2011, MetaQuotes Software Corp.

on the four-hour GBP/CHF chart. Notice how this trendy kangaroo has all the standard kangaroo tail features except for the "room to the left" rule. The tail sticks out beyond the nearby candlesticks, but because the market is in a strong downtrend, there is little room to the left for the trendy kangaroo tail. Trendy kangaroo tails will rarely have room to the left because they occur during trends, so there will always be price action to the left. The trendy kangaroo tail should, however, stick out beyond the recent choppy price action. Otherwise, the standard kangaroo tail rules apply. Notice the open and the close of the trendy kangaroo are both in the bottom third of the candlestick. The open and the close of the trendy kangaroo are inside the previous candlestick's range. The very next candlestick trades higher than the high of the trendy kangaroo, triggering the buy

FIGURE 10.7 This bullish trendy kangaroo on the four-hour GBP/CHF chart has many of the standard kangaroo-tail characteristics.
© 2000–2011, MetaQuotes Software Corp.

stop. The trendy kangaroo maintains all the characteristics of the standard kangaroo tail trade; the only difference is that it prints after a pause during a strong market trend.

You may notice that the daily AUD/JPY trendy kangaroo set-up (Figure 10.8) is not on a zone. This makes the trendy kangaroo unique; it is a naked trading set-up that is not always found on a zone. However, under most circumstances a minor zone will be seen at the market pause immediately before the trendy kangaroo. Notice how the highs of these candlesticks cluster near the bottom of the trendy kangaroo tail. Thus, the consolidation of candlesticks before the trendy kangaroo tail establishes a minor zone, and the bearish trendy kangaroo tail extends above this minor zone. Obviously, ideal trendy kangaroo setups will line up with a major zone, but this is not necessary.

BEWARE THE TRENDY KANGAROO TRAPS

Once you get the hang of the trendy kangaroo, you may want to trade them all the time. These trades do not occur frequently simply because the market does not trend that frequently. Be careful. There are many trendy-kangaroo-looking set-ups that are not ideal. Here are a few of the common mistakes naked traders make when looking for trendy kangaroo set-ups.

Trendy kangaroos must stick out from the consolidation range. If the trendy kangaroo candlestick does not have a tail that sticks out from the market pause, it is not an ideal trendy kangaroo (see Figure 10.9).

The best trendy kangaroos will print during a pause in the market trend. If a trendy kangaroo prints after a large correction, it may be a sign

FIGURE 10.8 This bearish trendy kangaroo tail on the daily CHF/JPY does not print on a zone. However, the candlesticks immediately to the left of the trendy kangaroo tail have similar highs, and thus they define a minor zone.

FIGURE 10.9 Trendy kangaroos should stick out from recent price action. Trendy kangaroos among other candlesticks are not high probability trades. This candlestick on the AUD/JPY daily chart does not stick out beyond the consolidation range, so it is not an ideal trendy-kangaroo trade.
© 2000–2011, MetaQuotes Software Corp.

that the trend is over. Beware of trendy kangaroos that print after a large correction, they may not be ideal trendy kangaroo trades (see Figures 10.9 and 10.10).

Trendy kangaroos are a great way to jump on a strong trend. Here are some things to keep in mind when looking at trendy kangaroos.

Characteristics of the bearish trendy kangaroo:

- The market is moving in a downtrend.
- The market pauses and several candlesticks print in a small consolidation range.
- A trendy kangaroo prints above the consolidation range.
- The stop loss is placed above the candlestick high.

FIGURE 10.10 The one-hour USD/CHF chart has a bullish trendy kangaroo tail. However, the market has fallen too far. The best trendy kangaroo tails print after a pause, this trendy kangaroo tail is not ideal because it has printed after a severe market correction.

© 2000–2011, MetaQuotes Software Corp.

- The sell stop is placed below the candlestick low.
- The market trades lower than the low of the bearish trendy kangaroo.
- The closest zone is the profit target.

Characteristics of the bullish trendy kangaroo:

- The market is moving in an uptrend.
- The market pauses and several candlesticks print in a small consolidation range.
- A trendy kangaroo prints below the consolidation range.
- The stop loss is placed below the candlestick low.

- The sell stop is placed above the candlestick high.
- The market trades higher than the low of the bearish trendy kangaroo.
- The closest zone is the profit target.

Optimal trendy kangaroos have these characteristics:

- The tail of the trendy kangaroo sticks out from the consolidation range.
- The trendy kangaroo prints on a major zone.
- The market does not make a large correction before printing the trendy kangaroo.

Live trendy kangaroo-tail updates are at www.fxjake.com/book.

After some testing, you may become comfortable with the trendy kangaroo. Remember that the goal for the trendy kangaroo is to capture a market trend after the market decides to pause. If you keep this goal in mind you will find that the trendy kangaroo is an excellent method for jumping on a strong trend. In Chapter 11 you will learn other exit strategies for capturing profits during trending markets; these may be ideally suited for trendy kangaroo-tail trades.

CHAPTER 11

Exiting the Trade

There's a trick to the Graceful Exit. It begins with the vision to recognize when a job, a life stage, a relationship is over—and to let go. It means leaving what's over without denying its value.

—Ellen Goodman

There are six stages for every trade you take. The first stage is the analysis: You take a look at the charts and decide whether a trade should be taken. The second stage is the planning stage: You decide if you will take a trade, and now is the time to develop a trading plan. You will place your order to enter this trade at a certain price, and you will place your exit for the trade at a certain price, whether it be at a loss or gain. The third stage of every trade involves the entry: the price at which you begin your journey on the trade. This price may have been predetermined; you may have decided that you will enter the trade if the market goes to a certain price, or perhaps you just use a market order and enter the trade immediately at the current market price. The fourth stage involves managing the trade, this is where Market Biofeedback™ comes in, and you are anticipating and reacting to the market data that comes back to you via the chart while you are holding your trade. The fifth stage is the exit. This is the most important stage of the trade. You make your money when you make your exit and your paycheck is received. The sixth and final stage is a learning phase. This is where you examine your trade from beginning to end and give yourself a grade. This may be automated learning (you simply dump your trade information into a spreadsheet such as the one available for you at www.fxjake.com/book) or it may be a more discretionary

TABLE 11.1 Six Stages of the Trade

Stage	Action	Goal
One	Identify the trade opportunity	Weigh risk to reward
Two	Create a trading plan	Follow trading system rules
Three	Enter the trade	Enter the market at a price that confirms the value of the trade opportunity
Four	Manage the trade	Use Market Biofeedback to adapt to new market information
Five	Exit the trade	Make money from the trade
Six	Learn from the trade	Identify weaknesses in stages 1–5

examination of your trade in the form of the trading journal, a place where you can write down your ideas about your trade.

In each of the six stages, you have an important goal (Table 11.1). In the first stage, your goal is to determine if the risk is worth the reward. In the second stage, your goal is to create a trading plan that you will stick to for the duration of the trade. In the third stage, you are attempting to enter the trade at a point where the odds are in your favor. In the fourth stage, your goal should be to maintain an open mind and to learn from the market information available on the chart. In the fifth stage your primary purpose is to make money. In this chapter we examine several ways of making money on profitable trades; some of these methods may make sense to you and others may not. It is important for you to choose one that fits with your ideas about the market. In the sixth stage, the goal is to improve your trading by learning from each of the previous five stages. In this way you can identify which of the previous five stages is your weakness. Many traders find the fifth stage incredibly challenging. For most traders, deciding on an exit strategy (and, more importantly, sticking to this exit strategy while managing the trade) is the most difficult aspect of successful trading.

EXITING WITH MONEY

The trade exit is the fun part; this is where your money is made. As a trader, this is your payday. When it comes to exits, all traders fit into one of two camps, runners and gunners. Runners and gunners are competing philosophies, and most traders will clearly identify with one or the other. It is important for you to decide right now before you read any further whether you identify with the runners or the gunners. The easiest way to determine which camp you fall into is to think about your answer to this question: Is it more important for you to have a high win rate or is it more important for you to have huge winning trades?

If you would rather have a high win rate, then you will probably have relatively small winners. You may have a high percentage of winners, but the average winning trade will probably be relatively small. If this is your style of trading, then you are a gunner. This is in contrast to the runner because if you are a runner, then you prefer to have huge winning trades. This means that many of your trades may end up as losing trades, or break-even trades, but the few giant winning trades will make up for these losing trades. Runner or gunner, it does not matter which is your style. It is only important that you stick to your chosen style of trading, stick with what you believe. You must trade in a manner that makes sense to you.

Runners

The runners are those traders who are looking out for the next big thing. These traders want to capture a large chunk of profit every trade. These traders have a strong sense of confidence. This confidence is unwavering and will not diminish in the midst of a losing streak. The runners are always hopeful that the next trade will end up as a beautiful, long-lasting trade. The long-running trades are what make profitable trading possible for the runners. Runners look at strong trending charts and think "now that is a trend that I would love to capture."

Runners understand that most of the time the market will not run in an extended trend. Runners are aware that a trading system may not have a high win rate. Runners wish to capture as much profit as possible, but they admit that it is unknown how far the market may move after entering a trade. Runners acknowledge that the market may not move very far, but once in a while the market may go very far and accelerate in a trending market. Therefore, the win rate is not the most important statistic for runners. Runners are much more excited about the profits that come with the long-lasting trades that capture a trending market. The patience exhibited by runners is extremely difficult for the other group to understand. Gunners have an altogether different perspective on trading.

Gunners

Gunners are a different breed. Winning is everything to gunners. Perhaps many gunners have a difficult time sitting through losing streaks. Or, it may be that gunners find it difficult to watch a trade go from profit to a break-even result. It may be that gunners are more impatient than runners, but in the end it really does not matter.

Gunners may also find profit in naked trading. Gunners, like runners, may decide to trade the kangaroo tail, the big belts, or any other naked-trading strategy. However, gunners are interested in quick satisfaction. Patience may not be one of the defining traits for gunners. Gunners understand that under normal circumstances the market is often moving up and down, up and down. Gunners believe the chances of capturing a strong trend are often quite minimal. This is why gunners are fine with small, consistent profits that they extract from the market. After all, gunners understand that these small profits will quickly add up.

EXIT STRATEGIES

By now, you understand the respective philosophies of runners and gunners. It does not matter if you decide to adopt the gunner philosophy and find consistent quick profits in the market or if you decide to side with the runners and try to capture a trending market for huge profits. The important thing is that you understand what makes sense to you and that you adopt and maintain this exit strategy in your trading. The first two exit strategies are for the gunners: the zone exit and the split exit. The second two exit strategies are for the runners: the modified split exit and the three-bar exit.

Exits for Gunners

Gunners are interested in quick profits. Gunners want to get in and out of a trade, and gunners *love* winning trades. The zone exit and the split exit are designed to take profits at the most important spots on the chart—the zones. Recall that the zones are those spots on the chart where the market repeatedly reverses. There is another characteristic of the zones that is important for the naked trader.

Zones are also magnets: The market tends to be attracted to these places on the chart. In other words, zones are simultaneously price barriers and price magnets. Exits based on zones take advantage of the fact that zones attract price.

Zone Exit   The zone exit is the basic exit for the naked trader. The naked trader looks to initiate trades at zones, and the naked trader looks to exit trades at these same zones. The basic philosophy of the naked trader is this: The market tends to bounce off zones repeatedly, like a pinball. Therefore, it is perfectly reasonable to look to these zones as potential profit targets. These zones are the most important places on the naked trader's chart.

Take a look at Figure 11.1, a one-hour chart on the EUR/JPY. By now, you will recognize this as a bearish big shadow. A sell stop below the low of the bearish big shadow netted 48 pips using the simple zone exit. Notice, also, that it only took two candlesticks to achieve this profit target.

Here is another example of a zone exit, this time it is the GBP/JPY four-hour chart in Figure 11.2. Again, you will now be familiar with the trade set-up. In this case it is a bullish kangaroo tail. With a buy stop entry placed just above the high of the bullish kangaroo tail, the target is achieved within four candlesticks. This trade made 86 pips.

It is important to note that the zone exit is extremely easy to implement, and it may be applied when the trade is initiated. In other words, you will know when you place your trade order exactly where the exit will be. There is no managing the trade, there is no need to watch the trade, and,

FIGURE 11.1 This is a bearish big shadow on the EUR/JPY one-hour chart. Using the zone exit, this trade makes 48 pips within two candlesticks, a very quick profit. © 2000–2011, MetaQuotes Software Corp.

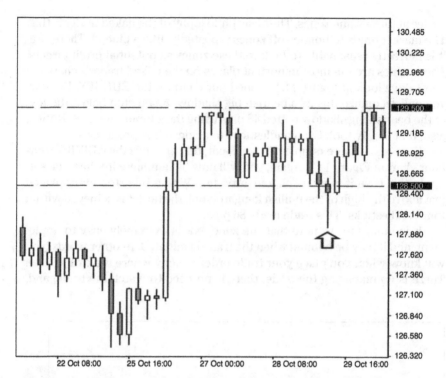

FIGURE 11.2 The bullish kangaroo tail on the GBP/JPY four-hour chart makes 86 pips four candlesticks after the trade is triggered. Notice how the market immediately reversed after reaching this zone. The zone exit enables the naked trader to avoid many losing or break-even trades simply because the profit target is often close to the entry price.

© 2000–2011, MetaQuotes Software Corp.

therefore, this is a nice trade exit for you if you do not sit and watch the charts.

Sometimes the market will get very near a zone, and then trade away from the zone. For this reason it is important that you place the profit target *near* the zone, with sufficient cushion. For sell trades, the profit target should be several pips *above* the nearest zone, and for buy trades the profit target should be several pips *below* the nearest zone.

In Figure 11.3 you can see where this rule enabled the naked trader to exit this trade with a profit.

The zone exit is a powerful exit, and many gunners find it easy to apply this exit. The split exit will often enable a quick profit, so it is ideal for traders who do not have the patience to wait through a long trade.

FIGURE 11.3 The AUD/USD four-hour chart shows a nice bullish kangaroo tail. This trade made 69 pips because the profit target was a few pips below where this zone was drawn on the chart. Placing a profit target precisely on the zone would have meant missing out on a profit and watching the market fall down and go against the trade.

© 2000–2011, MetaQuotes Software Corp.

Split Exit   The problem with the zone exit is that often the market will go much further than the first zone, and this may lead to frustration. Even gunners like to have trades that extend for a long time. The split exit is, therefore, a compromise that gunners may use to allow for the market to go a bit further than the first zone. Like the zone exit, the split exit may be used by those naked traders who are interested in hands-free trading.

To use the split exit, the naked trader must divide the trading position into separate positions. One simple way to do this is to divide the trade in half. So, for instance, if a trade has six lots, a split exit would mean using one target for three lots and a different target for the other three lots.

This is how a split exit is executed: The first zone, the nearest zone to the entry price, is used as a profit target for half the position, and the next closest zone is used as a profit target for the remaining position. Once the market achieves the first profit target, at the nearest zone, the stop loss is moved to break even for the remaining position. This obviously reduces the risk for the remaining position. The position will either hit the second profit target or it will be stopped at breakeven.

An example will illustrate how the split exit should be used. In Figure 11.4 there is a bearish kangaroo tail on the AUD/JPY one-hour chart. The market quickly falls to the first zone, 30 pips away, and so half the position bags 30 pips. The remaining half of the position becomes risk-free because the stop loss is now moved to the entry price. The market does retrace, but it does not make it back to the entry price. The market instead falls further, all the way down to the second zone, where the remaining position exited for a profit of 65 pips.

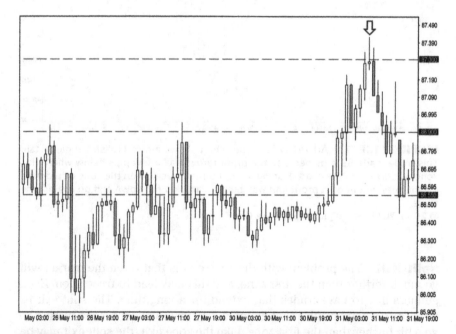

FIGURE 11.4 The AUD/JPY one-hour chart prints a bearish kangaroo tail on an important zone. Using the split exit, the naked trader is able to find 33 pips of profit on the first zone, and an additional 65 pips of profit at the second zone below the entry price.
© 2000–2011, MetaQuotes Software Corp.

The split exit will not always make additional profit. Some of these trades will end up with a smaller win simply because the market will come back and close out the remaining position at breakeven. In Figure 11.5, the AUD/NZD daily chart offers a bearish kangaroo tail on a zone. Using a split exit with this trade, the naked trader finds a profit of 73 pips at the nearest zone, but afterwards the market moves higher and hits the breakeven stop loss.

The split exit will require more patience than the zone exit. The fact remains that some trades will be stopped at breakeven when following the rules of the split exit. However, obviously, some trades will also make it to the second zone, and, therefore, the average size of the winning trades will increase. The split exit is, in essence, a compromise, a compromise for the gunners. Most gunners will be unable to apply the exit strategies that are appropriate for the more patient runners.

If you are a gunner but would like to increase the size of your average winning trade, the split exit may be the exit for you. If you are thinking that both the zone exit and the split exit do not take advantage of the strong trending moves that you observe in the markets, you are probably

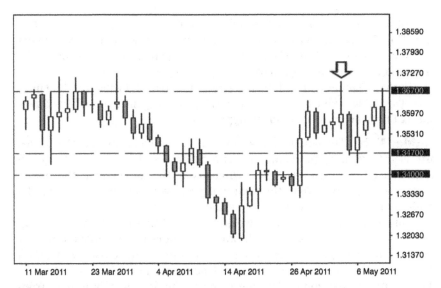

FIGURE 11.5 The AUD/NZD daily chart prints a bearish kangaroo tail on an important zone. The split exit enables the naked trader to make 73 pips at the first zone, but the market retraces beyond the entry point for a break-even result on the remaining trade.

© 2000–2011, MetaQuotes Software Corp.

thinking like a runner. Read the next section to see how runners approach their trading exits.

Exits for Runners

Runners see things a bit differently. Runners love bagging the big trade. Runners have incredible confidence in their trading systems. Runners are in it for the long haul. Runners use exit strategies to take advantage of trending markets.

The first exit for runners is similar to some of the gunner exits. This exit is called the ladder exit. The second exit for runners is a little bit different because it is not based on the zones. Both of these exits are classified as trailing exits, which simply means that they take advantage of trending markets.

TRAILING EXITS

An exit strategy that is dynamic, with no fixed exit price. The exit price constantly adjusts with the movement in the market to maximize profit.

All trailing exits are a compromise. There are two parts to the trailing exit. The trailing exit must allow a cushion so the market may move against the position, and the trailing exit must have a line in the sand to capture the profit once the market moves too far against a position.

Both the ladder exit and the three bar exit do best during trending markets. The ladder exit uses zones to identify profit targets, whereas the three-bar exit uses an entirely different approach.

Ladder Exit   The ladder exit is similar to the previous exits in that zones are used to identify profit targets. The difference, however, is that each zone is a potential profit target. When using the ladder exit, the naked trader never knows *where* the final exit price will be; this is because the ladder exit allows the market some breathing room.

This is how the ladder exit works: Once a trade is initiated, the stop loss is moved in accordance with how far the market has moved. So, for example, if the market moves from the entry price to the closest zone, then the stop loss is moved to breakeven. Once the market moves further to the second closest zone to the entry price the stop loss is moved from breakeven to the first zone, and so forth. The easiest way to see how the ladder exit is executed is to look at an example.

Figure 11.6 is the GBP/USD four-hour chart. A bearish big belt prints on the 1.6460 zone. The market trades down to the 1.6270 zone, so the stop loss is moved from the high of the big belt candlestick to breakeven.

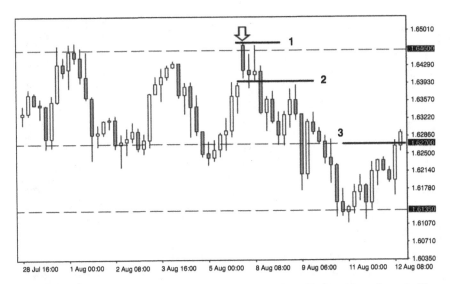

FIGURE 11.6 This is a bearish big belt on the GBP/USD four-hour chart. 1. The stop loss is above the high of the bearish big belt. 2. The stop loss moves to breakeven once the market reaches the first zone. 3. The stop loss moves to the first zone once the market reaches the second zone, this is where the trade is exited for 128 pips.
© 2000–2011, MetaQuotes Software Corp.

Then the market hits the next zone at 1.6135, so the stop loss is moved to the 1.6270 zone. The market turns around and trades back up to the 1.6270 zone, where the trade is exited for a gain of 128 pips.

Patience is needed to employ the ladder exit. Take a look at Figure 11.7. This is another example of the ladder exit on the EUR/USD weekly chart. Here we see a bullish kangaroo tail. The market immediately trades higher than the kangaroo tail and reaches the first zone at 0.8750 quite easily. At this stage, the stop loss is moved to breakeven. The market trades higher to reach the zone at the 0.9100 level. Here, the stop loss is moved to the first zone down at 0.8750. Next, the market makes a move higher and reaches the next zone at 0.9330, so the stop loss is moved to the second zone at the 0.9100 level, and this is where the trade is exited for a gain of 575 pips.

Using the ladder exit will allow the market a "cushion" of one zone. This may seem frustrating, to allow the market to come back and stop out a trade for less profit, but this is the nature of the trailing exit. All trailing exits (including the three-bar exit described further on), have to allow some breathing room, or "cushion" in order to capture the large profits available in trending markets.

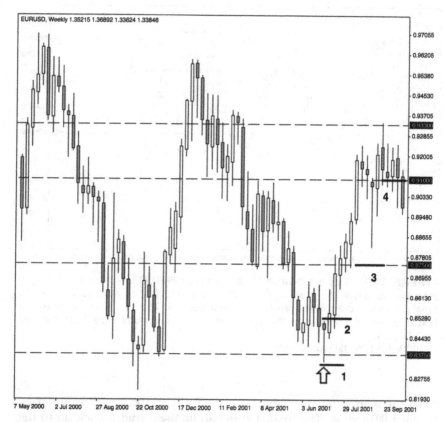

FIGURE 11.7 The ladder exit on a weekly EUR/USD bullish kangaroo tail. 1. The stop loss is first placed below the low of the kangaroo tail. 2. The stop loss is moved to breakeven once the market reaches the 0.87500 zone. 3. The market trades up to the next zone at 0.9100, so the stop loss is moved to 0.8750. 4. The market reaches the next zone at 0.9330, so the stop loss is moved to 0.9100, and this is where the trade is exited for 575 pips.
© 2000–2011, MetaQuotes Software Corp.

Three-Bar Exit   The three-bar exit is a unique exit because, unlike the previous exits, it does not involve zones. The three-bar exit gets its name because the exit is based on the price action of the most recent three bars (or candlesticks). The exit is a simple trailing exit based on the lowest low of the previous three candlesticks (for buy trades), or the highest high of the previous three candlesticks (for sell trades).

The naked trader locks in profits by trailing the stop loss behind the lowest low (for buy trades) of the previous three candlesticks. Take the example on the one-hour GBP/AUD chart. This trade is obviously a bullish trendy kangaroo on an excellent zone at 1.5868 (see Figure 11.8). The initial stop-loss placement is below the low of the trendy kangaroo.

Once the market prints three candlesticks after the trendy kangaroo, the stop loss is moved below the low of the lowest candlestick. The lowest of the three candlesticks in Figure 11.9 is the third candlestick, the candlestick immediately after the trendy kangaroo candlestick. The stop loss is moved to just below the low of the candlestick immediately following the trendy kangaroo candlestick.

In Figure 11.10, the three-bar exit is applied to GBP/AUD one-hour trendy kangaroo. One more candlestick prints, and so the stop loss is moved higher, this time it is placed below the third most recent candlestick because it has the lowest low at this stage of the trade.

In Figure 11.11 the market moves higher once again after another one-hour candlestick closes. The GBP/AUD one-hour trendy kangaroo is trending nicely, and the three-bar exit is locking in profits as the market trades higher.

The one-hour chart for the GBP/AUD changes drastically as the market makes a strong move downward (see Figure 11.12). At this stage, the candlestick with the lowest low is the most recent candlestick, so according to the three-bar exit rules the stop loss must be placed a few pips below this most recent candlestick.

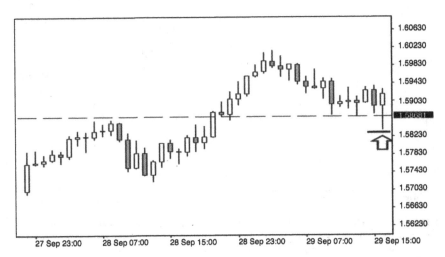

FIGURE 11.8 The stop loss for the GBP/AUD one-hour trendy kangaroo is first placed below the low of the candlestick.
© 2000–2011, MetaQuotes Software Corp.

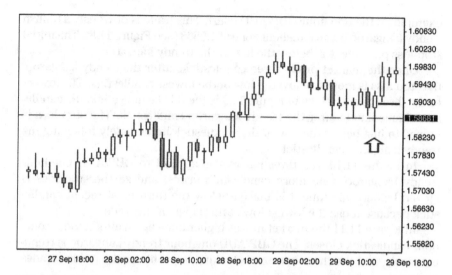

FIGURE 11.9 The three-bar exit applied to the GBP/AUD one-hour chart. Once the market has printed three candlesticks, the stop loss is moved beneath the lowest low of the most recent three candlesticks.
© 2000–2011, MetaQuotes Software Corp.

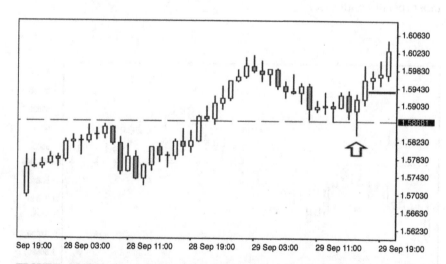

FIGURE 11.10 The three-bar exit applied to the one-hour GBP/AUD trendy kangaroo trade. The market moves higher, and the stop loss is placed just below the lowest low of the three most recent candlesticks.
© 2000–2011, MetaQuotes Software Corp.

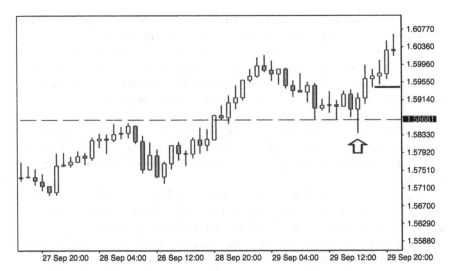

FIGURE 11.11 One more candlestick prints, and the three-bar exit is adjusted once again. This time the third most recent candlestick is again the candlestick with the lowest low, so the stop loss on the GBP/AUD trendy kangaroo trade is placed below the third candlestick.
© 2000–2011, MetaQuotes Software Corp.

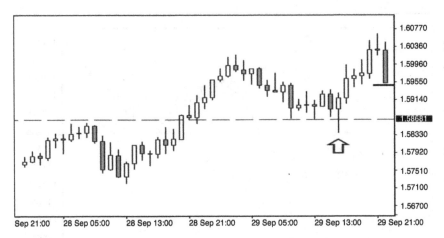

FIGURE 11.12 The most recent candlestick on the one-hour GBP/AUD chart makes a strong move down. The stop loss is placed below this candlestick because it has the lowest low of the most recent three candlesticks.
© 2000–2011, MetaQuotes Software Corp.

One more candlestick prints, and the trade survives by a whisker. The new candlestick is slightly lower than the previous candlestick, so the stop loss is placed below this most recent candlestick (see Figure 11.13).

The next one-hour candlestick on the GBP/AUD one-hour chart (see Figure 11.14) prints slightly higher. The stop loss remains at the same location because this second candlestick still has the lowest low of the most recent three candlesticks.

The one-hour trendy kangaroo trade on the GBP/AUD chart is closed out on the next candlestick (see Figure 11.15). The most recent candlestick pushes through the stop loss, and so the trade is closed for a modest gain of 13 pips.

Some of the trades that are managed according to the three-bar exit will end up with similar results to this GBP/AUD one-hour trendy kangaroo trade. The three-bar exit is ideal for a strong trending market, but if the market does not continue moving with a strong trend, the three-bar exit will only capture minimal profits. Although this may seem discouraging for some traders (particularly gunners), for runners, who take a long-term perspective, a few losing trades or minimal gains are acceptable. Runners understand that the large gains will come from time to time and make the three-bar exit a worthwhile exit strategy.

Another example of the three bar exit is in order. This time, it is the AUD/JPY daily chart, and the trade set-up is a bearish big shadow (some

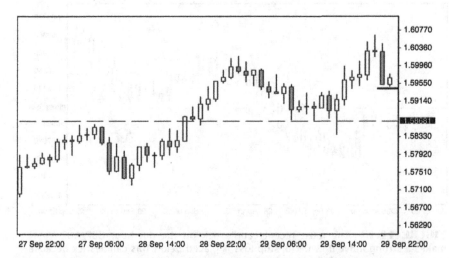

FIGURE 11.13 The GBP/AUD one-hour trendy kangaroo trade survives after the next candlestick prints on the chart. This most recent candlestick now has the lowest low, so the stop loss is placed a few pips below this candlestick.
© 2000–2011, MetaQuotes Software Corp.

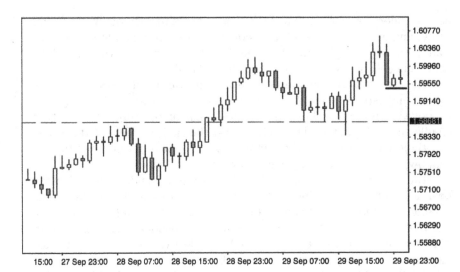

FIGURE 11.14 The stop loss for the one-hour GBP/AUD trendy kangaroo trade remains the same because the most recent candlestick does not present a lower low.
© 2000–2011, MetaQuotes Software Corp.

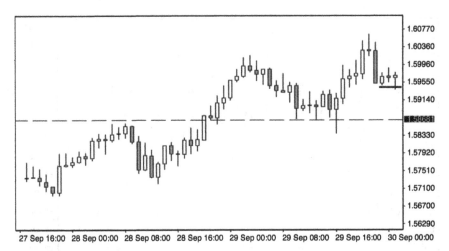

FIGURE 11.15 The next candlestick triggers the three-bar exit stop loss. The most recent one-hour GBP/AUD trades low enough to hit the stop loss, and so the trade is over after a gain of 13 pips.
© 2000–2011, MetaQuotes Software Corp.

naked traders may argue that this set-up is not a bearish big shadow, but something else; go to www.fxjake.com/book to watch a video about this trade). The original placement for the stop loss is just above the high of the bearish big-shadow candlestick (see Figure 11.16).

The stop loss remains above the high of the big shadow until three more candlesticks print after the bearish big shadow. The stop loss is moved a few pips above the highest high of the three most recent candlesticks. As Figure 11.17 illustrates, the highest high of the previous three candlesticks is the candlestick immediately following the big shadow, so the stop loss is placed above this candlestick.

The next chart (see Figure 11.18) shows four candlesticks after the bearish big shadow. The highest high of the most recent three candlesticks becomes the most recent candlestick. Therefore, the stop loss is placed a few pips above the high of the most recent candlestick. It is important to note that according to the rules of the three-bar exit, the candlestick must close before the stop loss may be moved.

Another candlestick prints and the candlestick with the highest high remains the same. The stop loss is not moved because the second most recent candlestick still has the highest high (see Figure 11.19).

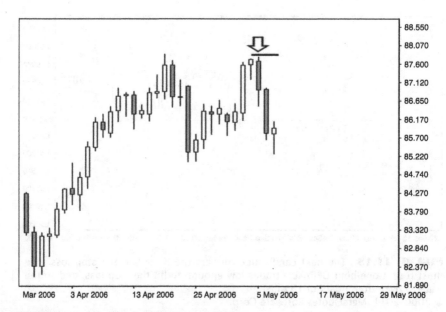

FIGURE 11.16 The initial stop-loss placement for the daily AUD/JPY bearish big shadow is just above the high of the big shadow.
© 2000–2011, MetaQuotes Software Corp.

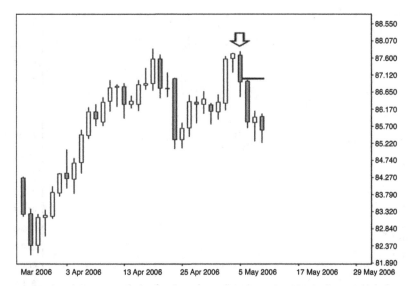

FIGURE 11.17 According to the three-bar exit, once the third candlestick prints the stop loss may be adjusted. In this case, the first candlestick after the AUD/JPY daily bearish big shadow has the highest high of the three candlesticks, thus the stop loss is placed a few pips above this candlestick.
© 2000–2011, MetaQuotes Software Corp.

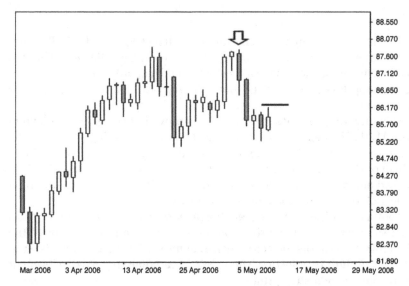

FIGURE 11.18 The most recent candlestick on the daily AUD/JPY chart becomes the candlestick with the highest high. Thus, according to the three bar exit, the stop loss is placed a few pips above the high of the most recent candlestick.
© 2000–2011, MetaQuotes Software Corp.

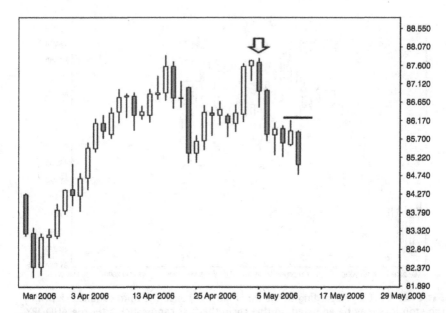

FIGURE 11.19 Using the three-bar exit, the stop loss placement on the AUD/JPY daily bearish big shadow trade remains the same after one more candlestick prints. © 2000–2011, MetaQuotes Software Corp.

The next day, the market takes another fall (see Figure 11.20). The stop loss remains the same, above the third most recent candlestick. The two more recent candlesticks have lower highs, and, according to the three-bar exit, the stop loss placement is above the highest high of the prior three candlesticks.

This time the stop loss for the trade is moved once again as shown in Figure 11.21. The next candlestick prints and the highest high becomes the third most recent candlestick, so the stop loss is placed a few pips above the high of that candlestick. When using the three-bar exit, if the stop loss is placed above the third candlestick, then it is known that after the next candlestick prints, the stop loss will be moved.

Another candlestick prints, and the highest high is once again the third most recent candlestick, so the stop loss is moved a few pips above the high of this third candlestick as is seen in Figure 11.22. Again, since the stop is above the third candlestick, there will be another stop-loss adjustment once the next candlestick prints.

One more candlestick prints, and the new highest high is the most recent candlestick, so the stop loss is placed a few pips above this candlestick (see Figure 11.23).

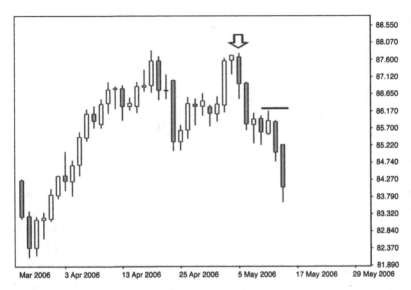

FIGURE 11.20 The market makes another move down, but the stop-loss placement on the AUD/JPY daily bearish big-shadow trade remains the same. The stop loss remains a few pips above the high of the third candlestick.
© 2000–2011, MetaQuotes Software Corp.

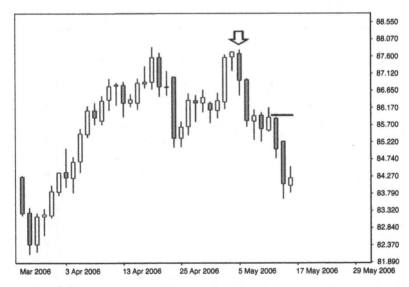

FIGURE 11.21 The market prints another small candlestick and the AUD/JPY trade has a new stop loss placement above the third most recent candlestick, according to the three bar exit rules.
© 2000–2011, MetaQuotes Software Corp.

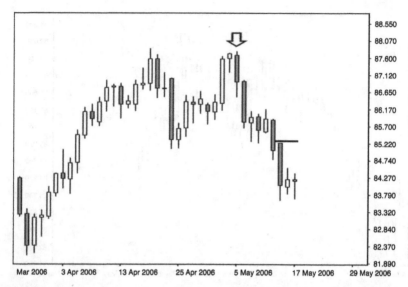

FIGURE 11.22 After a new candlestick prints, the stop loss is placed a few pips above the third most recent candlestick, the candlestick with the highest high of the previous three candlesticks.
© 2000–2011, MetaQuotes Software Corp.

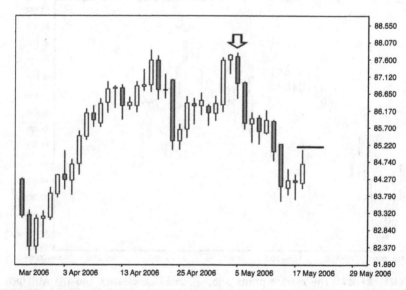

FIGURE 11.23 The most recent candlestick has the highest high of the three most recent candlesticks, so according to the three-bar exit, the stop loss is placed above this candlestick.
© 2000–2011, MetaQuotes Software Corp.

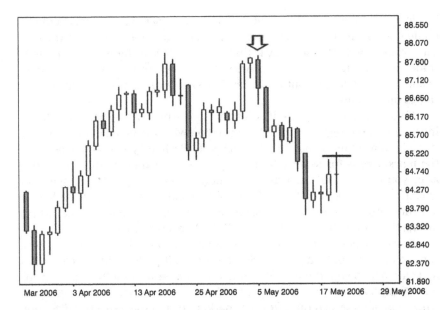

FIGURE 11.24 The most recent candlestick trades through the stop loss. The bearish big-shadow trade on the daily AUD/JPY chart has captured 137 pips.
© 2000–2011, MetaQuotes Software Corp.

The market has finally triggered the three-bar exit shown in Figure 11.24 and the trade is over. The most recent candlestick takes out the stop loss. This bearish big shadow on the AUD/JPY daily chart has netted 137 pips by using the three-bar exit.

The three-bar exit works best when the market accelerates into a strong trend. As long as the three most recent candlesticks are following the trend, the three-bar exit will trail slightly behind the advancing candlesticks, capturing profit along the way. This exit is ideal for runners who are interested in capturing large profits.

At times, the three-bar exit may be frustrating, some trades will end up as losers, other trades may give back much profit, but if used consistently, this trailing exit will capture big moves. The key to this exit is to use it *consistently, for every trade.* Runners are like all traders: They never know when the next big trend will pop up. But gunners who apply trailing exits such as the three-bar exit are ready to capture profits from the next trend in the markets.

MANAGING EXITS

A common problem for traders is *re-trading* the most recent trade. This issue is extremely common for traders struggling with an exit strategy.

Traders will take a close look at a recent trade, see where improvements could have been made, and then decide to change things for the next trade. The problem with this strategy is that every trade is different. The previous trade has nothing to do with the next trade. Every trade is an independent event. When traders fall into this trap of *re-trading* the previous trade, bad things often happen.

If you have found yourself adjusting your strategy in general, or changing your exit strategy in particular, based on what occurred in the previous trade, you are falling into this trap as well. Perhaps you take a trade and the market runs for several hundred pips in the expected direction, long after you have exited the trade. This may encourage you to change your exit strategy on the next trade. The problem with this is the next trade may not run for several hundred pips, and may only go to the next zone, which means that you will reduce your profitability even further.

Decide which type of trader you are going to be. Either you will be a runner, or you will be a gunner. Stick to one exit philosophy. Decide what makes sense to you. If you are a gunner do not get upset if the market runs for 500 pips after you exit the trade. If you are a runner do not get upset when you get stopped out after the market goes in the expected direction initially. It is important to stay true to your trading beliefs. The best way to do this is to avoid *re-trading* the last trade. In fact, *re-trading* the last trade may send you into a cycle of doom—never a fun place for traders. In the next chapter we examine this cycle in detail.

PART THREE

Trading Psychology

CHAPTER 12

The Forex Cycle

Insanity is doing the same thing over and over again but expecting different results.

—Rita Mae Brown

It is true that most traders do not consistently find profits; the vast majority of forex traders lose money consistently. Because of this, many traders find it difficult to stick with a trading system. The vast majority of traders are always looking for a new and improved trading system. The trading system gets the blame for all the losses. Most traders are, therefore, constantly searching for a better trading system, looking for a solution to the consistent losing. The ironic thing is that the solution has nothing to do with the trading system.

An explanation of the cycle of doom will help you to see how you can break out of this cycle if you are currently finding it difficult to reach consistent profits.

WHAT IS THE CYCLE OF DOOM?

The cycle of doom consists of three phases. The first phase is the search. The second phase is the action. And the third and final phase is the blame. A close look at each of these phases reveals that the cycle of doom characterizes a logical approach to trading. To become a successful trader, however, you will have to break out of the cycle of doom.

How do you break the cycle of doom? The first step is to understand the cycle. Once you understand the cycle of doom, you may break free from the cycle of doom. It is important for you to understand what is happening so that you may identify it, and then move beyond the cycle of doom and into the world of consistent, profitable trading.

Phase 1: The Search

In this phase you are searching for a trading system. You may look for your trading system in trading books, in online trading forums, trading education websites, or you may find your trading system from speaking to another trader at a conference or meeting. In the end, it is not important where you find a trading system, only that you find a trading system that appears to be successful.

If you are unable to find a trading system that you are comfortable with, then you're probably in phase 1. You will leave phase 1 only once you find a trading system that is truly exciting, a system that you look forward to trading. In fact, phase 1 of the cycle of doom is complete once you find a trading system that you simply *cannot wait* to trade. The defining feature of phase 1 is that the trading system *is* the solution. Once you have found a trading system that is exciting, you will move beyond phase 1.

Phase 2: The Action

Phase 2 is the action phase. This is the fun part; you begin to trade your system. If you are like most traders, you will leap into phase 2 with just about every trading system that looks decent. The excitement of using a new trading system is irreplaceable. This excitement comes from the *unknown* (more about this later). Will this new trading system work? Will you become a billionaire trading this system? Is it everything you hope it to be?

Amid this excitement you begin to trade the system with high hopes. It is highly unlikely, given that you are extremely excited to start trading your new system, that you would have time to test your trading system. The proof for your new trading system is so overwhelming that there is no need to test the trading system. If you do decide to test your trading system before jumping into the action phase, congratulations, you are a member of the cautious minority of traders.

This is the exciting phase because you're able to put your trading system to the test. You may not have decided to test your trading system before moving into the action phase. In fact, only a small percentage of traders do test a trading system before moving into the action phase. This action phase is punctuated by excitement. It is exciting to trade a new system, not knowing what may happen. You may find that the trading system does well for an extended period of time. Perhaps you find that optimism abounds. However, at some stage things look bleak. Maybe profits pour in early, but eventually the losing trades pile up.

A drawdown eventually appears. There are several losing trades in a row. These trades may have appeared just as you decide to increase the risk per trade. Obviously, this was an ill-timed modification to your trading system. Just as you decided to increase the risk per trade, the system ran into a bumpy road. This drawdown is the beginning of the end of phase 2. This drawdown will mean that you lose faith in your trading system, and begin to move into the next phase.

Phase 3: The Blame

Phase 3 is the blame. The blame is the phase in which the trading system is scrapped. Because the trading system has not found consistent profits, you decide to dump the trading system. The trading system is at fault. The trading system found the losing trades. The trading system must be responsible for the drawdown. Frustration sets in because the system that looked so fool-proof ended up being a loser. You decide it is time to move on to a new trading system.

Return to Phase 1

The cycle of doom is punctuated by a return to phase 1 after phase 3. Once you have completely given up on your system, you decide to find another system, a better system. The search is on again. The cycle repeats itself once again (Figure 12.1).

The cycle of doom makes sense to the trader who is convinced that profits come from trading systems. The problem is this: Profits do not come from trading systems. Profits come from traders. Traders find profits in the

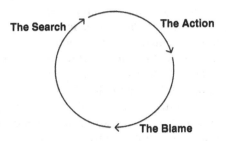

FIGURE 12.1 Most traders find it difficult to break out of the cycle of doom.

markets, and the tool (trading system) used to extract these profits is not as essential as the trader's execution. The fatal mistake that most traders make is to assume that trading systems are responsible for profits.

LIVING IN THE CYCLE

The cycle of doom may be familiar to you; it is certainly familiar to me. I was stuck in the cycle of doom for years. Losing consistently is no fun, I should know, I did it often. It may be difficult to believe, after spending years trading and losing, that it is possible to reach the land of profits; however, it is possible to achieve consistent profits trading forex. The first step toward profitability is identifying that you have been stuck in the cycle of doom.

A close examination of how many traders approach trading reveals that the cycle of doom is due to how traders approach their trading, and not the viability of a trading system.

Another way to look at this is to consider that two traders may be trading using the same system. One trader is consistently finding successful, profitable trades, and the other trader is consistently losing money. What is the difference between the two traders? They both trade using the same system. The difference is in the trader.

The key to breaking the cycle is to recognize that the trading system is not responsible for trading profits or losses. *You* are responsible for trading profits and losses.

DEFEATING THE CYCLE

It is possible to defeat the cycle of doom. I have done it, and many other naked traders have also broken the cycle. You can certainly defeat the cycle of doom. You must want to become a professional trader. If you want to trade consistently, and if you want to find profits, it may be best for you to stick to a trading system that you believe in.

One way to gain confidence in your trading system is to back-test it. You already know this. Have you done it? Have you tested any of the trading systems in this book? If you have not, perhaps you are not ready to defeat the cycle. But do not lose hope, for there may be another opportunity for you to find confidence in your trading. There may be a very good reason why you have not back-tested any of these systems at this stage.

It may be that you are waiting for a trading system that resonates with you. Perhaps once you find this trading system you will be able to go and test it extensively, and build your confidence in this trading system before using it in a live market. If this sounds like you, then the next chapter is for you. You are the type of trader who must create your own trading system. You must trade a system that is completely yours. This is fine, you are in good company, and there are many traders who, like you, must trade only a homegrown system. Trading your own system may be the best way to avoid the cycle of doom, and this is explored in detail in the next chapter.

CHAPTER 13

Creating Your Trading System

*My parents taught me how to listen to everybody be-
fore I made up my own mind. When you listen, you
learn. You absorb like a sponge—and your life becomes so much better than when you are just trying
to be listened to all the time.*

—Steven Spielberg

Years ago, I met a trader named Miguel. He, like many others before him, was interested in becoming a full-time forex trader. We spoke about trading psychology, trading systems, reasons for becoming a professional trader, and we talked about how boring trading is. My friend was a professional in the finance world, who worked at a bank in Switzerland. He really wanted to learn how to trade for consistent profits in forex. I told him that once he learned to be an efficient trader, his trading would become very boring. He was shocked to hear this. It is true, successful trading often *is* boring. He did not believe me, but nevertheless he thought it would be great if he became a bored professional forex trader.

Many years later, my friend has left his job at the bank, moved from a chilly country to a nice, warm tropical location, and he now trades a few times each month. He wrote to me to say, "Now I know what you mean when you said that 'trading will become boring.'" I hope this happens for you. I hope that trading becomes boring. I hope that you do the same thing over and over and over again, and find it very easy to pull profits out of the forex market. If you work hard, your trading may become boring. The key is to define who you are as a trader. Once you do that, you may put a plan to action that will allow your trading to become boring.

So, how will you define your system? The answer lies in who you are. Who you are will define how you trade. What makes sense to you as a trader may not make sense to me. This is fine. There are many ways to find profits in forex. If a trader tells you there is only one way to make profits in forex, he is wrong. There are *many* ways to pull consistent profits in forex. You simply have to find your way.

WHAT DO YOU BELIEVE?

Your beliefs will drive your trading. If, for example you believe it is impossible to make money scalping, then you will have a very difficult time making money scalping. If this is your belief, focus on longer-term charts.

The Rules

The rules of your trading system will define how you interact with the market. It may seem like this is a very small detail, but in fact it is the definition of the game. Those traders who do not have rules—and many traders enter the market without rules—are simply gambling. It is important for you to define what your system rules are, if only for the fact that having them in front of you will help to remind you that you have a method for extracting profits. Beyond that, it is important for you to remember that your system rules also define what you should do in *any* situation. Your entries, your exits, your trade management and your risk strategy should all be contained in your system rules.

It may be tempting to create a system without precisely defined rules, but know this: A well-defined trading system is more likely to withstand your personal psychological attacks against your trading system. Less interpretation often means better trading, and the best-defined systems are "just-this" resistant. If you have experience trading you know how tempting it is to modify your trading system *just this* time, or perhaps you have found yourself willing to override a trade signal your system offers *just this* time, or maybe *just this* time you have decided to move your stop loss to give a trade a little more breathing room. *Just-this* trading leads to disasters, and it is important for you to develop a trading system that is just-this resistant.

Are You a Market Specialist?

The first decision to make when designing your system is to decide which pairs, which markets you will be trading. All the systems contained in this book will work on many markets, and most timeframes. The question becomes this: Which type of trader are you? You may decide between two basic trader profiles. The first is the market specialist. As a specialist you will concentrate on one market. There are many successful traders who do just this. Perhaps you only want to trade the EUR/USD. If you decide to be a EUR/USD specialist, you will learn the intricacies of the pair. Each market has a personality, and as a EUR/USD specialist, you will learn the personality of the euro. You might also learn the correlations associated with the pair, when the pair is reacting in an unusual way, and so forth.

At the time of the writing of this book, Ashkan Bolour, a professional forex trader who is very familiar with the EUR/USD market, had discovered a very peculiar correlation. Bolour has been exploiting this correlation with a scalping strategy for over one month. He had determined that the EUR/USD had been closely following the Dow Jones Industrial Average. By waiting for the Dow to establish a direction for the trading day, he knew precisely which direction to scalp the EUR/USD. He said, "I don't know how long the correlation will last, but for now it does make a consistent profit."

Now it is important to note that, as a market specialist, you will probably uncover similar relationships such as this one in your trading. Remember that these relationships will not always last; they are transient. Although it is great to exploit these relationships, you must always be on your guard when they start to fall apart.

As a market specialist, you will discover relationships such as the one Bolour used in his trading. You will become familiar with the market, you will know what it does around the nonfarm payroll report, you will know when the interest-rate announcements are for your market, and you will be aware of what the currency pair is likely to do. In general, you will have a feel for your chosen market. This is the great advantage.

Some traders begin trading with the belief that they must trade every market available, and that simply is not the case. Market specialists are some of the most profitable traders on the planet, and many of them have an exceptionally high win rate. This comes with the understanding of the market and having an intimate relationship with the market, the factors that affect the market, and a method for determining the mood of the market. If you think that becoming a market specialist is for you, then make sure that you back-test your chosen trading system extensively on your market. You may be surprised at what you find.

Market specialists will sometimes use several different trading systems on the same market. Perhaps you decide you want to become a market specialist and work only with the GBP/USD. This may mean that you are using several trading systems on the GBP/USD. For example, you may decide to trade daily kangaroo tails on the GBP/USD. You may also decide that you are going to take last-kiss trades on four-hour GBP/USD charts.

As a market specialist, you may even find that you are simultaneously long and short (buying and selling) your currency pair, simply because you are trading multiple timeframes and strategies. This may seem confusing or unlikely, but if you choose to follow the path of the specialist, you may find it makes sense to follow the short-term and long-term impulses of your chosen market simultaneously. Perhaps buying your market on the one-hour chart, and selling it on the weekly chart.

These seemingly contradictory positions make sense only to the market specialist, the trader who has intimate knowledge of the market he trades.

Are You a Trade Specialist?

If the idea of trading one market does not appeal to you, then you may want to consider the alternative: becoming a trade specialist. As a trade specialist, you will focus on one trading set-up, it may be the moolah trade or big belts, or perhaps trendy kangaroos. The set-up you choose does not matter, you must simply be comfortable trading the system. You will gain comfort trading this set-up across markets by back-testing. Obviously, this will involve back-testing. It is only through back-testing that you can accumulate experience and confidence in your trading set-up to apply it across markets consistently and repeatedly for profits. Additionally, to become a trade specialist, you must get comfortable with all phases of the trade.

All trades are similar to a good story, they have a beginning, middle, and an end. In the beginning, the question is: Do you want to take this trade? Is the risk for this trade worth it in your mind? Have you seen similar set-ups in the past that have worked out? If you feel as though you simply *must* take the trade, because it is too good to be true, then you should take a trade. The beginning, in some ways, is the most difficult part of the trade. The beginning phase of your trade is when you act as a filter. You are filtering out those subpar trading set-ups. You, as a trade specialist, know precisely what those grade-A set-ups look like. This will obviously come from your back-testing. You will have gained experience through your accumulation of knowledge; this only comes with exposure to charts, which only comes with trading live accounts and demo accounts and back-testing. Based on your trading experience, you will know which trades to filter out. This is the most important and critical phase of the trade as a trade specialist.

The second part of the trade occurs when you are managing the trade. This is where Market Biofeedback™ comes in. Does the market provide any critical information about the trade? How do you feel about the trade, given the price action that has printed *after* entering the trade? When the market tells you what to do, make sure you are ready to act on this information. Disregarding market information is stubborn trading. If you join the group of stubborn traders who hold onto beliefs despite contradictory market information, you too may find them to be very expensive beliefs (see Chapter 16 for more on expensive beliefs).

The third and final part of the trade is the exit. Now, your style of exit strategy is obviously something that is unique and special to your personality. You simply must trade and exit in a way that make sense to you, and fits with your view of the markets. The exit is where the money is made. Exits literally discriminate traders; traders who consistently make money know how to apply exits. Those traders who consistently lose money usually have great difficulty with exits.

If you doubt that exits control your trading destiny, then consider this: Have you taken the exit challenge? (Learn how to test the power of exits at www.fxjake.com/book). If you have, you have seen the power of exit. By applying an exit strategy, you are able to consistently pull profits, regardless of why you have entered. If you have done the exit strategy challenge, then you know how powerful a proper exit strategy, if applied consistently, will bring home money consistently. It is not too late to do the exit strategy challenge, so if you have not tried it, please do it. It is a great way to put the exit in perspective.

As a trade specialist you will become familiar with each phase of the trade for your chosen strategy. You will learn how to discriminate good set-ups from poor set-ups, you will learn how to discern if a trade is going well, or if it is not going well, and you will learn how to apply your chosen exit strategy consistently. (Note that all trades may experience a drawdown, but the experienced trader, a trader who understands Market Biofeedback, will know when to pull the plug on a trade that is poorly performing)

You will have to back-test your chosen specialty, to build your confidence, and become an expert with your trading system. Experience trading your system across a broad range of markets is important if you are to apply this system confidently and consistently. You may find, for example, that, as a specialist trading the last-kiss trade, it works extremely well on the four-hour charts and the daily charts, but when you apply it to the one-hour charts, the win rate plummets for you. This is valuable knowledge, and instead of trying to fight the system, knowing how you trade it, and which timeframes are effective are important pieces of information that you can use to improve your trading and aid your success.

Choosing Your Timeframe

Choosing your market is important—just as important as choosing your timeframe. There are three questions to answer when considering the timeframe you are willing to trade. First, what type of person are you? Your trading personality will go a long way to determine the timeframe that you will feel comfortable trading. Second, how much time do you have during your day? Traders who have considerable time to trade may be able to trade lower time frames (such as the five-minute or fifteen-minute charts), but people with very busy days may not be able to trade anything other than the higher timeframe. Third, are you a patient trader? Patient traders will be able to endure the inevitable fluctuations in longer-term trades, but impatient traders find it very difficult, and end up trading shorter timeframes. In fact, impatient traders make very good scalpers.

Before you decide on your chosen timeframe, remember these two principles: First, the shorter the timeframe you decide to trade, the more intense concentration you will need to sustain to be consistently profitable. Second, as a rule, traders who start out trading longer timeframes and trade those timeframes successfully for months (or years) have a much higher success rate than those traders who jump straight into the five-minute charts. So choose your timeframe carefully.

RISK RULES

Trading is simply a game of managing risk. How many trades will you take at any one time? How large will your trading positions be? When thinking about risk, there are three key aspects you should consider: (1) your risk appetite, (2) maximum drawdowns, and (3) correlated trades.

Risk Appetite

The simplest rule to apply is to think about your sleep. If you are able to put a trade on, place the orders in your platform, and then go to sleep, this is the trade size that fits your risk profile. If, however, when you place a trade you find it difficult to sleep, you find that you are always thinking about the trade while away from your computer, then the trade is too big. You need to reduce your trading to the *sleeping point*, the point at which you can place a trade, accept the risk, and get a good night of sleep.

SLEEPING POINT

The point at which you can place a trade, accept the risk associated with the trade, and get a good night of sleep. If a trade is constantly on your mind or if you find yourself checking a trade at odd hours in the night, there is too much risk associated with the trade, and it should be reduced to the sleeping point.

Maximum Drawdown

Your appetite for risk will help determine the size of your trade, but so will your maximum drawdown. The maximum drawdown is the amount you are willing to lose over a period of time. An easy way to track the maximum drawdown is to look at it from the point of view of one trading week. For example, you may risk 1 percent of your account on each trade. If you set your weekly maximum drawdown to 5 percent, you can withstand five losing trades in a row. After five losing trades, you have hit your maximum drawdown for the week. You may decide to stop trading once your maximum drawdown is hit.

How you decide to apply the maximum drawdown rule may depend on the timeframe you decide to trade. You may decide to have a maximum drawdown per month if you trade a longer timeframe. If you trade shorter timeframes, you may decide to have a maximum drawdown amount for one day. It is up to you to decide. Note that your maximum drawdown will affect how many trades you are able to take at any given time.

For example, you may decide to have a maximum drawdown of 5 percent for each trading week. If you have six daily trade signals on the first trading day of the week, and you risk 1 percent on each of these trades, you could have a drawdown of 6 percent should all those trades go bad at once. The implication, of course, is that you should reduce your risk so you are unable to reach your weekly drawdown on the first day of the week if all of the trades end up losers. So, if you have a 5 percent drawdown rule per trading week, and you have six trading signals in one day, perhaps instead of risking 1 percent per trade you risk 0.65 percent per trade for an overall risk of 3.9 percent. This way, you have another 1.1 percent to risk the rest of the trading week should all 6 trades become losers.

Another critical question you must ask about your trading system is this: How will you deal with drawdowns? Will you use a stop-trading rule? How will you recharge your batteries and jump back into trading after a drawdown? Perhaps you believe that a "drawdown retreat" is a good idea. You may decide to get away from the charts, and, if possible, get away from your trading station and take a trip out of town after experiencing a drawdown. The theory behind this is if you get away from trading for a while you will (1) avoid revenge trading (a quick way to blow up your account), and (2) come back to the charts with a fresh perspective.

The best way to come back to the charts fresh is to simply follow a planned sequence whenever you experience a maximum drawdown. For example, you may decide to follow this five-step sequence: (1) *Go away*. You will get away from your trading station and away from your home or trading office. Even if only for the weekend or couple of days. It is important to remove yourself from the place where you have experienced the drawdown. (2) *Back-test your system*. This should be a predetermined number of trades (e.g., 200 trades) or a set time period (e.g., EUR/USD daily chart from 2009 through 2011). (3) *Evaluate your trading statement*. What has been working well? What has not been working well? Is the drawdown due to bad luck? Or is the drawdown due to a lack of discipline; are you following your trading rules? Perhaps there are a few currencies that account for 85 percent of your losses? Take a good look at your trading statement to see what seems to be working and what needs improvement. Make sure that you go back far enough with your statement to see what was working for you *before* the drawdown. (4) *Decide if your system still works*. You have back-tested and you have examined your trading statement. If your trading statement reveals nothing more than bad luck, and back-testing suggests your trading system still works, it is time for another test. Test your trading system on *recent market data*. This way you can be sure that your trading system no longer works. If your drawdown has occurred over the past three weeks, take a close look at recent market data from the past three months to see if the system is profitable. If you have found that the system is no longer profitable, it might be best to stick to a demo account when you begin trading again.

DEMO ACCOUNT

Short for "demonstration account"—many forex brokers offer free practice accounts, also called demo accounts. These accounts allow forex traders to become comfortable with the trading platform (the broker's trading software), and they also allow traders to test trading systems with real markets. These accounts will keep track of winning and losing trades because they are funded with an amount of simulated money such as $50,000.

Demo trading will ensure that you do not lose money if the trading system no longer finds consistent profits. You must be careful of jumping back into the cycle of doom when doing this. If your trading system no longer turns a profit (and you are applying the rules consistently), it is time to find another system. (5) *Work on you*. You are the most critical aspect of your trading system. When your confidence is shaken after a serious drawdown you should transition back into trading carefully. The goal should be to build up confidence. The two easiest ways to build confidence are to back-test your system (see it working over historical data) and to create a positive mindset. (Specific tools for improving your trading psychology are covered in Chapter 16.)

Decide and plan for your approach to a drawdown. Nearly every trader will have to sit through one of these difficult times. Professional forex trader Ashkan Bolour suggests that there is always time for making money in the markets. He says, "If something is not working, step away, re-analyze your trades, and *then* come back to the markets. Stepping away from the markets will give your mind and your body time to rest, and you will be much better for it when you come back to the markets."

Coming out of an extended drawdown your goal should be to slowly build up your confidence. It is necessary to have a regimented routine for getting through these drawdowns. Without a strong structure, without rules designed to keep you from emotional revenge trading after a drawdown, you're almost certain to fall into undisciplined trading and to take on excessive risk. Design a plan today so that if a drawdown appears, you are ready for it, because you will not feel like designing a drawdown plan in the midst of a drawdown.

Correlated Trades

Correlated trades are perhaps the most obvious threats to your trading account. For example, from time to time the markets may print daily kangaroo tails on many of the yen pairs. If I decide to take the daily kangaroo tail on the USD/JPY, AUD/JPY, NZD/JPY, CAD/JPY, EUR/JPY, and GBP/JPY, I must be careful. What will happen if each of these trades are available on the same day, and I have a maximum drawdown limit of 5 percent for the week? With a risk of 1 percent per trade, I quickly reach my weekly drawdown limit simply by taking these trades should they all end up as losing trades.

One obvious solution is to reduce the per-trade risk when several correlated currency pairs offer trading set-ups. If you have a background in statistics, you understand what a correlation is, but if you do not understand correlation very well, take a look at the correlation video at www.fxjake.com/book. You will learn how to measure the correlation between any two currency pairs. Once you have determined that two currency pairs are correlated, the next step is to reduce your overall risk for correlated trades.

Here is an example of a plan for managing correlated, simultaneous trades.

Bullish kangaroo tails print on the daily charts for the following pairs: USD/JPY, AUD/JPY, NZD/JPY, CAD/JPY, EUR/JPY, and GBP/JPY.
The standard risk per trade is 1 percent.
The maximum weekly drawdown is 5 percent.
For simultaneous trades with a correlation of 0.65 and above, the risk is reduced to 0.5 percent per trade.

The correlations are run on the six currency pairs and all are correlated above the 0.65 level, so the overall risk per trade is set to
0.5 percent, for an overall risk of 3 percent on the day.

Even if all six trades end up as losers, the drawdown will only be 3 percent, so there will be 2 percent of additional risk available for the
week (two standard trades at 1 percent risk each).

Decide how you will manage the risk on correlated pairs. As with every
other aspect of your trading plan, if you decide on a plan of action *before*
you are in the midst of a high-pressure trading decision, you and your trading account will be much better off.

MANAGING YOUR TRADES

The way you manage your trades is completely a personal decision. There
are two parts to managing the trade. The first part is managing the entry
price. The second is managing the exit. Both decisions may be personalized
depending on the way you decide to approach your trading.

As for the entry price, there are several possible methods of entering
a trade. You may take a market order (executing the trade at the current
market price). You may take a limit order (executing the trade after the
market retraces, or moves in the "wrong" direction). Or you may decide
to use the recommended buy stops (or sell stops for sell trades), executing the trade entry only once the market moves in the expected direction.
Additionally, you may also decide to use an alternative entry strategy: You
may wait for the market to offer a clue. In other words, you enter your
trade once you receive market feedback, once the market suggests it will
move in the expected direction.

Managing the exit is also critical. There are many exit strategies available to you, many of them listed in Chapter 11. However, you may also
decide to manage your exit based on market activity.

Some traders believe that all trading decisions should be made before
the trade is triggered. In other words, the entry price, the stop-loss placement, and the profit targets are all determined in the beginning, *before the
trade is initiated*. This way, there is no thinking after the trade is triggered.
Traders who adhere to this philosophy attempt to get out of the way, and
allow the market to rate the trade as a winner or loser. Some traders take
this approach because they have jobs outside of trading. This restricts their
availability for managing the trade. This limited exposure to charts can be
a good thing. Sometimes traders get in the way.

Traders may get in the way during the analysis of the markets, when decisions are made concerning which trades to take. Many traders have found that too much market analysis is counterproductive. It is often easier and more efficient to have a quick look at the markets, decide on a course of action, and then to simply set the trades and forget them.

Abe Cofnas, a renowned trader who deals in both spot forex and forex options, has this to say about market analysis: "It is so fascinating to see—but for me I often find my best trading results occur when I do minimal analysis, and let my visual sense of price action let me react to and not anticipate conditions."

Cofnas is certainly not alone. There are many traders who follow this same philosophy. Sometimes traders can simply out-think themselves, and it may also come during the exit phase of the trade. Colin Jessup, a naked forex trader in Canada has this to say about managing his trades: "If price action retraces more that 61.8 percent towards my stop, I will close the trade to minimize the loss. Usually the 70 percent level is my line in the sand if I'm watching a trade live. That said, due to my schedule, my trades usually either hit my target or stop me out."

Decide for yourself how much management you will do when trading. Stick to these rules. Try to duplicate your back-testing in your live trading. This will ensure that your live trading results will resemble your back-testing results.

Managing Stops and Profits

How will you take losses? Will you wait for the market to hit your stop loss or will you close out the trade manually before your stop is hit? Will your profit targets be achieved automatically, or will you wait to see if the market can push through a zone before exiting?

Are you a runner or a gunner? If you are a runner, your stop loss and your profit target may be one and the same (for example, if you are using the three-bar exit). If you are a gunner, will you leave your profit targets in your trading platform and walk away?

Your disposition and your lifestyle will probably answer these questions for you. If you are at work during the day and are unable to manage your trades, you may need to let your trading platform do the managing for you. If, however, you are a full-time trader or have access to your charts nearly all day long, be careful. It may seem like a good idea to be able to watch the charts all the time; it may seem like a good idea to have your trades available on your phone at all times. Sometimes watching your trades unfold may mean you exit a trade prematurely. The rule of thumb here is to trade your system just as you back-test it. You must make sure that your back-testing duplicates how you will trade in your everyday life. If you get very nervous watching your trades, then it is probably best that you walk away. It may be best for you to let your trading platform manage your trade if you find yourself making poor decisions when watching the live markets.

The forex trading platforms today are brilliant, and they offer many opportunities for trailing exits, the ability to move a stop loss based on market action, and so forth. Know who you are as a trader, and what your weaknesses are. If you find yourself doing better, capturing more profits when you step away to allow your trades to either hit the take profit or the stop loss, without your intervention, perhaps you should stick to this hands-off approach to managing your trades. Perhaps you are able to manage your trades successfully and cut your losses before they hit the stop loss. The important thing to remember is that a few poor trades do not mean you should redesign your trading system (beware the cycle of doom).

Using Market Information

The market is constantly sending information to market participants. What will you do with that information? Will you take market data and use it to adjust your entry strategy? Will market information help you to manage your exits?

For example, if you're looking at taking a bullish kangaroo tail, you may decide to place your buy stop above the high of the kangaroo tail. But what if the market trades down to the stop loss level before the buy stop entry is triggered? Does this mean that you will disregard this trade and remove your pending buy stop order? See Figure 13.1 for an example of this scenario on a one-hour GBP/USD kangaroo tail set-up.

If the market pushes through where the stop loss would be, it may make sense to cancel the trade. This is using market information to manage your trades, even before they occur. You may also use market information to manage your exits.

If you are in a trade and the market prints a reversal signal, how will you react? If you are in a sell trade and the market prints a buy signal, will you exit a trade? Will it depend on where the reversal signal prints? Some naked traders will only close a trade if the market prints a reversal signal on a zone. Other naked traders will simply close a trade as soon as price action offers a counter signal, a signal in the opposite direction of the trade. Decide how you will manage a reversal signal. If you are in a buy trade and the market gives a sell signal, will you exit?

Take a look at the daily NZD/USD chart in Figure 13.2. This is a sell signal, a bearish kangaroo tail on the 0.7590 zone. The market triggers the

8 Aug 23:00   9 Aug 03:00   9 Aug 07:00   9 Aug 11:00   9 Aug 15:00   9 Aug 19:00   9 Aug 23:00   10 Aug 03:00   10 Aug 07:00   10 Aug 11:00

FIGURE 13.1 The GBP/USD prints a kangaroo tail on the one-hour chart. However, instead of pushing through the buy stop order, the market falls lower than where the stop loss would be. Most naked traders will cancel the buy stop in this situation.
© 2000–2011, MetaQuotes Software Corp.

trade and falls, as expected. However, once the market reaches the zone at 0.7430, an interesting candlestick prints. This is *not* a bullish kangaroo tail because the open is not inside of the previous candlestick's range. Nevertheless, the candlestick does suggest that the market has found support down here at 0.7430, and thus the naked trader may decide to close out the position.

Decide how you will use market information. If you are very comfortable interpreting price action, perhaps you will use market information to adjust your trade as the candlestick prints on the chart. For many traders and those new to naked trading, it may be easier to simply stick with your trading plan and let your trade reach the profit target or the stop loss.

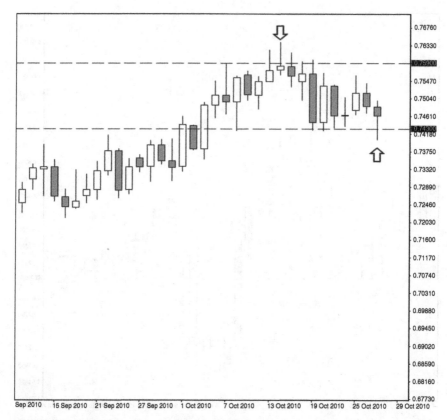

FIGURE 13.2 The daily NZD/USD chart prints a bearish kangaroo tail, suggesting the market may fall. The market does fall, but once it reaches the next zone at 0.7430, a bullish "almost kangaroo tail" prints, suggesting the market may move higher.
© 2000–2011, MetaQuotes Software Corp.

KNOWING YOUR TRADING PERSONALITY

The most important factor in determining how you will trade is your trading personality. What is your trading personality? How do you know what you do best, and how do you know what is uncomfortable for you? The basic distinction among traders is the one that distinguishes short-term scalpers from longer-term swing traders. You probably already know which camp you belong to. If you find it difficult to go to sleep or walk away from your charts knowing that you have money at risk, then you either (1) have too much at risk for your trade or (2) you are not fit for trading longer-term charts. Likewise, if you find it nearly impossible to sit through a trade on the five-minute charts, watching your equity seesaw back and forth, you are probably best suited to the longer-timeframe charts. What makes sense to you?

Do you like to take trades with the flow of the market, or do you like to find reversal points? Take the *Trading Personality Quiz* to find out which trading systems fit your view of the markets at www.fxjake.com/book.

Typically traders fall into one of two categories: (1) "go with the flow" trend traders and (2) reversal traders. The trend traders are drawn to the runners' exits in Chapter 11, and the reversal traders often enjoy trading for profit targets. You may remember this group from Chapter 11—the gunners. Remember that you may not have the patience to stick with the trade and ride out a long-lasting trend if you are a reversal trader, quick profit targets may be more your style. If you are a trend trader you will have to learn to deal with those trades that fall back and end up as breakeven or losing trades, even after they start out in profit.

Trade what makes sense to you. If you think it is easier to find turning points, trade reversals. If you think it is easier to ride the trend, make sure you get good at identifying and riding strong trends.

Your Life, Your Trading

How often you trade is an absolutely critical decision, Trading can deplete your psychological and physiological energy. If you don't believe this, then consider this: The next time you have an exceptional trade, a trade that bags several hundred pips, once you close the trade try to immediately make another trade. Will you find it easy to make another trade? Of course not! The reason is that trading is draining, and you must take care of yourself.

As a trader, you must be physically fit. A healthy body equals a healthy mind. To stay healthy, you must get more than adequate sleep, you must take good care of your body. You must try to *limit* your time in front of a computer screen. If you fail to do these things, your trading will suffer. You can even make a game out of it. Perhaps you decide that you are only able to trade if you do some exercise that day. Or, perhaps you decide that if you do not get at least seven hours of sleep, you are not allowed to trade the following day. The idea here is to set goals to encourage good habits.

One habit to avoid as a trader is drinking and trading. It may seem like an obvious pitfall, but if you do drink, avoid trading under the influence. Just as you would not want to drink alcohol and go for a drive, you certainly do not want to drink a bottle of wine and then decide to scalp the GBP/USD for a few hours. As a forex trader, you are well aware of the fact that the market is nearly always open. For many traders it can be tempting to trade into the wee hours of the night. If you are under the influence, it is best to avoid making any trading decisions.

Good habits should extend into the psychological realm. If you enjoy self- hypnosis or meditation, you may find that your trading improves drastically when you consistently find time each day to practice self-hypnosis or meditation. (There are more resources for you at www.fxjake.com/book if you would like to learn more about meditation or self-hypnosis.) Perhaps you decide to take some time each day to mentally recharge before you make your trading decisions, before you sit down and analyze the charts.

If you are thinking right now "I do not need to spend any time being quiet; I just do not have time for that," please at least consider a new approach to your trading. For one month try using self-hypnosis, meditation, or just some simple quiet time alone before you jump into your trading routine. You may find your trading results improve. Something as simple as some quiet time alone can recharge your psychological batteries, and better batteries will mean better trading results.

Trading will suck the psychological energy from you if you allow it to happen, so be careful. Trading six plus hours per day is possible, but probably only for those people who are full-time traders. If you are trying to work a job and trade six plus hours each day, you are probably going to be an inefficient trader. You may make mistakes, find it difficult to concentrate, and find it difficult to stay consistently profitable if you are working a full-time job and working as a trader full-time. It may seem as though trading is a wonderful, carefree life, but it is *work*.

How Subjective Is Your Trading?

The last important facet of your trading system is how much room for interpretation you are allowing in your trading system. Do you decide to take only those trade set-ups that look right? Or do you take only those trades that are strictly defined by your trading system?

Each trader takes a different approach to the application of the trading system. For example, perhaps trader Elliott decides to trade the big-shadow set-ups on the daily charts. Elliott will only take those big-shadow set-ups that look to be very high-probability set-ups. The bearish big-shadow set-ups must have a close down near the low, and the bullish big-shadow set-ups must have a close near the high. The big-shadow candlesticks must be very large and Elliott decides to only take those big-shadow set-ups that trigger the entry price on the next candlestick, and he takes profit at the nearest zone. Elliott may believe that he is using a very strict, well-defined trading system, but if you ask Molly, she might disagree.

Trader Molly decides to also trade only daily big-shadow trades. Trader Molly takes a different approach. Trader Molly will only take big shadows that are larger than the previous five candlesticks by at least 15 percent. Trader Molly also decides to only take those big shadows with the closing price within 15 pips of the low (for bearish big shadows) or the high (for bullish big shadows). Molly consistently applies the three-bar exit to her strategy, knowing that she may have some losing trades and small winners, but she will also have a few large winners.

Where do you fall on the continuum? Are you more like Elliott? Do you prefer to trade with a little bit of subjective analysis? Or are you more like Molly? Perhaps you share her desire to have clear concrete trading rules so it is very clear what you should be doing when following your trading system.

Choosing Your Playing Field

In many ways, the timeframe you choose to trade is determined by your lifestyle. If you don't have four or five hours a day to sit down and watch the charts, it will be difficult for you to be a five-minute chart scalper. Unless you have an automated exit for your shorter-timeframe trading, it is unlikely that you will be able to trade the shorter-timeframe charts without several hours of screentime. Even if you do have an extra four or five hours each day, you may be better off avoiding trading the shorter-timeframe charts. Many traders have found it is much easier to simply take a look at the charts once a day, put in your trading orders, and then walk away. Sometimes, after a few years of this sort of trading, successful traders will move down to shorter timeframes. A general rule of thumb is this: Trading shorter timeframes means a smaller margin for error.

Trading the shorter timeframe means that you must be precise and decisive when executing your trades. An example will best illustrate why this is the case. If you decide to trade the five-minute EUR/USD chart in the hopes of pulling 10 pips of profit from the markets, then you are paying a high price to trade. The spread (the difference between the price for buying the EUR/USD and the price for selling the EUR/USD) on the EUR/USD is likely to be quite tight, perhaps two pips, so you must make 12 pips to bag 10 pips of profit. This is a commission of 16 percent (2 pips divided by 12 pips = 16 percent). This is a hefty commission.

If, instead, you are trading the daily EUR/USD chart, you may be looking to gain 100 pips and will need to capture 102 pips to cover the spread, so this is an overall commission of 1.9 percent—a significant reduction in the commission cost. Longer-term trading is not only cheaper, it is easier to execute successfully. If you initiate a daily chart trade and enter your trade at a poor price, perhaps you miss your entry price by 3 pips, you may, instead, make 97 pips, rather than the full 100 pips. This is a reduction of profits by 3 percent; not great, but certainly something your trading account can probably withstand. If this same type of poor execution is associated with a short-term trade, a 3 pip slip up becomes a reduction in profits by 30 percent (3 pips out of 10 is 30 percent). A consistent reduction in profits by 30 percent may tip the trading system over into the abyss of unprofitable systems.

It is your choice, you must decide if you have the trading experience, the time, and the mental toughness to consistently execute short-timeframe trades. If you do not have all three, it may be best to stick to the longer-timeframe charts.

Your Trading Lifestyle

As you can see, there is much more to your trading system that simply deciding on whether you prefer to trade the last kiss or trendy kangaroos, whether you like to trade the one-hour chart or the weekly chart. It is important for you to decide not only what you will trade, but also how you will trade it, and to define the precise rules you will use to trade your system. Defining all these variables for your system up front will help you down the track when you have to endure difficult times. Drawdowns, losing streaks, and bad luck are all more manageable when you have a well-defined trading system in front of you.

One last note should be made about your successes. When thinking about your trading system, much of your planning may involve reducing exposure to risk. However, you should also think about your successes. What will you do when you have an exceptional run? Will you take time off to celebrate? Will you pull some of your profits out to buy something nice for yourself? Remember to celebrate your wins.

DEFINING YOUR TRADING SYSTEM

In summary, creating your trading system involves several aspects. The following list will help you to refine your trading system and define the rules so that you are ready for any situation *before* it arises. If your trading system answers all these questions, you have done well, and you have a true trading system.

- Are you a market specialist or a trade specialist?
- How many hours of daily screen time do you allow yourself?
- Which trading session (European, Asian, or North American) do you trade?
- Which timeframes will you trade?

- Which trading set-ups do you trade?
- Which exit strategies do you use?
- How much interpretation do you have when placing trades?
- How much interpretation do you have when exiting trades?
- What is your maximum risk per trade?
- What is your maximum weekly drawdown?
- What is you maximum monthly drawdown?
- How do you deal with drawdowns?
- How will you regain confidence after a maximum drawdown?
- What will you do to ensure you are physically fit to trade?
- What will you do to ensure you are psychologically fit to trade?

CHAPTER 14

Becoming an Expert

Far too many people—especially people with great expertise in one area—are contemptuous of knowledge in other areas or believe that being bright is a substitute for knowledge.

—Peter Drucker

Forex traders around the world are making money every day. These traders have one thing in common—a secret. This secret may surprise you. If you are like me, when you first started learning about trading you thought all the traders who were making money were computer science, mathematics, or physics wizards with lightning-fast computers deploying secret algorithms. Trading was the domain of the well educated that had the computing power to crack the market code. I was convinced that only by duplicating these efforts would I be able to consistently rack up profits. I knew that trading had to be complex, and perhaps you feel think same way.

This is not true.

Some of the very best traders in the world share a simple secret: They use extremely simple and yet powerful, trading systems. The best traders in the world—hedge fund traders, bank traders, private millionaire traders you will never hear from—all have one thing in common: These people are experts. They do *one* thing.

WHY DO YOU WANT TO TRADE?

This may seem like a funny question, but why do you want to trade? If you want to trade because you want to make money, perhaps trading is for you. If, however, you want to trade because you want excitement, or you want to be able to tell people that you are a trader, or because you love the excitement of having money at risk, then perhaps trading is not for you. If you want excitement try skydiving, or hunting wild boars. If you want to tell people that you are a trader, you can do that, but if you are not quite consistent with your trading, just trade a very small account, that way you can get the recognition of being a trader for a small fee. If you love the excitement of having money at risk, you should try gambling. Gamblers are honest. They risk their money, and they recognize the inherent risk in their occupation, they are up front about it. This is an honorable approach to gambling because gamblers admit that their money is at risk and admit that luck will guide their winnings. Traders can be gamblers in disguise if they are trading for the wrong reasons.

You probably know a gambler or two disguised as a trader. This is the difference between a trader and a gambler: A gambler has no risk management, and a gambler is willing to lose large amounts of money quickly. A trader treats each trade as a calculated risk and manages each trade according to his system rules. Gamblers can lose all the money at once, and traders lose only as much money as their system will allow. The distinguishing factor is that a gambler does not follow risk management rules, whereas a trader follows strict risk management controls.

Expert traders do more than simply follow strict risk management controls; they also concentrate on one trading technique. This is the real secret of expert traders: They focus on one market, one trading system, one edge, and they use this edge in their trading repeatedly. Profitable trading is boring. Profitable traders are experts, and these expert traders do one thing over and over again.

THE SECRET OF THE EXPERTS

Why do profitable traders limit themselves? The answer is simple: Profitable traders know what makes money. Profitable traders trade to make money. If you would like to make money as a trader, do what the experts do. Become good at trading one system. You know how to do this now. All you need is in this book. You simply need to put the work in, practice, and become an expert with a trading system that makes sense to you, and then trade that trading system. Trade your system over and over again until trading becomes boring (and very profitable).

All the very successful traders are doing one thing. This may seem unbelievable, but entire hedge funds are built on one idea. Hedge-fund traders often have one edge, and they use this edge in their trading. Now, some hedge funds may have several traders, each with his own edge, but to be a successful trader you simply have to have one thing that you are very good at, and then you do this one thing over and over again.

The most successful traders I know follow this rule. The traders that struggle, the traders who have difficulty finding consistent profits, are the ones who repeatedly change their systems, reanalyzing and reorganizing their trading rules. In other words, they are still stuck in the cycle of doom. The key to breaking the cycle of doom is to decide what makes sense to you, which of the trading systems in this book resonate with you. Once you have chosen one, you simply need to test it over and over again. Then apply this system, concentrate on following your system rules, and watch your confidence grow.

You can do the same thing hedge fund traders do. You can be just like a bank trader. You can be a professional trader. But before you go pro, you must decide how you will make your money in the markets. What is your expertise? Which trading system fits your beliefs? Once you align your beliefs with a trading system, you simply need to gain experience and confidence in the trading system, and you will never look back. Your exciting journey is ahead of you; soon you will become an expert trader.

SIX STEPS TO BECOMING AN EXPERT

Although it may seem that becoming an expert is a very difficult thing to do, it is really rather simple. As with many things in life, if you put the work into it, you will be able to reap the rewards. Here are six steps to becoming an expert.

Step One: Get in the Comfort Zone

The first step is to become comfortable drawing zones on your chart. Zones are the basis for your trading decisions. As a naked trader, all your trading decisions will be based on zones, so it is very important that you have these zones drawn correctly on the chart. It is much easier to draw fewer zones, provided those zones are very strong and well defined, than it is to draw too many zones on your chart. If in doubt, err on the side of using fewer zones on your chart.

As a naked trader, you will spend a lot of time waiting for the market to hit your zones. This is fine; this is part of what it means to be a naked trader. If you find yourself feeling as though you need to take action, perhaps you should back-test your trading. Test one year's worth of data (on a shorter timeframe), and then test a lower frequency trading system on longer-timeframe charts. Compare the profitability of each back-test. Are you surprised at what you find? Sometimes making money is easier when you do not trade. Sometimes avoiding trades is just as important as taking trade opportunities when they arise.

> *Goal: Learn to quickly identify zones on any chart.*

Step Two: Decide on a Catalyst

The second step toward expertise is for you to decide on which catalyst you will use in your trading. You have learned about several catalysts (and there are more at www.fxjake.com/book), and hopefully by now you have back-tested some of them. So which one resonates with you? Do you prefer the simplicity of the kangaroo tail? Or do you like the added confirmation of the last kiss? Perhaps you find the trendy kangaroo to be an excellent method for capturing trending markets. It does not matter which catalyst you have chosen. What does matter is that you trade a catalyst that fits with your view of the markets.

You must trade a catalyst that fits with your beliefs. Choosing a catalyst that fits with your beliefs will help you to ride out any bumps in your equity curve and avoid the cycle of doom.

> *Goal: Choose the one trading catalyst that you want to build your expertise on.*

Step Three: Back-Test

By now you probably have a good understanding of all the benefits associated with back-testing your trading system. Back-testing will verify that your trading system works. It will help to build your confidence in your trading system. It will help you when you are experiencing drawdowns, it will help save you from falling back into the cycle of doom. In short, back-testing is what separates those consistently profitable traders from those traders who are forever stuck in the cycle of doom.

If there is one idea that you take from this book let it be this: Back-testing your trading system is the one thing that you can do to accelerate your trading. This one thing is the most important habit that you can develop in an effort to become a professional trader. Back-testing is that important.

You should have a clear goal in mind when you back-test your trading system. Try to triple your trading account with a small percentage at risk for each trade (e.g. 1 percent or 2 percent at risk). Tripling your trading account will help you to believe in your trading skills.

> *Goal: Risking 2 percent or less, triple your back-testing account.*

Step Four: Forward Test

If you have back-tested your trading system, and you are happy with the results, you're ready for the next step. The next step is to employ your trading system in real time. Unfortunately, this is a very slow stage. You will be unable to speed up time as you can when you are back-testing, but you will closely mirror the live market trading experience.

Create a goal for your forward testing. Try to triple your demo account. Because you will be trading in real time, it will probably take longer to triple your account than it did when you tripled your back-testing account. However, in some ways, demo trading much more closely resembles "real" trading because you cannot quickly advance the charts to see if you have made the correct trading decisions. Embrace the time it takes to accumulate expertise with your forward testing.

To forward test, you simply need to open up a demo account. These accounts are offered by any forex broker.

> *Goal: Risking 2 percent or less on each trade, triple your demo account.*

Step Five: Trade a Small Account

After you have found success back-testing and found success forward testing, it is time to start trading a live account. Live trading can never really be duplicated. Back-testing is wonderful and adds to your confidence; forward-testing is also great because it closely resembles live trading. However, the only thing that matters is live trading profits. Begin with a very small trading account. What is small to you may not be small for someone else. The size of your account should be made up of 100-percent risk money. This is money that you are willing to risk for this exercise. Never risk more money than you can afford to lose.

Once you triple this small account, you are ready. You have built your confidence by trading (back-testing with historical data, live data with your demo account, and, finally, you have tripled your small live account). At this stage, you probably cannot wait to begin trading your standard live account.

> *Goal: Risking 2 percent or less on each trade, triple your small account.*

Step Six: Trade a Live Account

Most traders do not do what you have just done. You have built your confidence over the previous five steps. Now you are ready. It is time to put into practice what you know, and by this stage you will be excited. Make sure that you maintain your discipline and continue to do the same thing that you have been doing. The important thing here is to follow your system, without regard to whether you are in the midst of a lucky streak or an unlucky streak.) Remember, you have the power of your trading, and you understand that you will successfully pull profits from the market.

The most important thing at this stage is to duplicate what you have been doing. Just because you are trading a standard account does not mean anything changes. Concentrating on your trading system rules will yield positive results. Thinking about the money involved in each trade will probably be distracting and will likely throw you off track. Keep doing what you do well, and you will become an expert.

> *Goal: Risking 2 percent or less on each trade, stick to your trading rules. Focus solely on following your trading system rules.*

DOING IT AGAIN

Is it possible to duplicate these steps with another trading system? If you have decided to follow the path of the market expert, you probably will add more systems to your repertoire. It is not necessary that you do so. It may be easier for you to trade one system comfortably for at least eight months before attempting to become an expert with another system.

Eventually, you may decide to do what many profitable traders decide to do. You may want to gain expertise with an additional trading system. It is not necessary to do so, and it may be tempting to jump headfirst into another system, but you should first give yourself time to get bored with your first system. There are at least two reasons for becoming an expert with a new trading system. The first is that trading the profitable system is boring. Perhaps it seems crazy to you that you may one day become bored with consistent trading profits, but it may happen. You may want to expand your horizons, and add another tool to your trading tool chest. The second reason for becoming an expert with a new trading system is based on risk management. By diversifying your trading strategy, you may reduce the likelihood of an extended drawdown. All trading systems have drawdown, but if you have a complementary trading system, one that is likely to make profits while the other is struggling, then you have the makings of a solid trading strategy. Many professional traders eventually get to the stage where trading diversified trading strategies makes sense. It is not necessary, of course, but it is possible for you to become an expert all over again with a new trading strategy. This *is* a great way to reduce your risk.

BORING TRADING IS EXPERT TRADING

If you find yourself bored with your trading, you are probably consistently profitable. The desire for change or a new challenge is often the biggest threat to profitable trading.

Exciting trading is often a sign of one of two problems. Either the trading system is new and unproven (not back-tested) or there is too much risk on each trade. If the system is unproven, the excitement is due to the unknown. This is not a good thing. Exciting trading is exciting because it is akin to gambling. Gambling is exciting. This is precisely why risking too much on any given trade is exciting. Trading should be fun, but if it is exciting. It is a sign that the system is unproven or you are risking too much.

Remember the story about Miguel? He is an expert trader, and by his own admission, his trading is boring. Embrace the day that your trading becomes boring. It may still be very fun to make money consistently, but it does not have to be exciting.

A SIMPLE TRICK

Right now you know how to become an expert. You know what you can do to get to expertise, it involves work, but if you choose to take the path of the expert, it is now available to you. The problem with the steps to expertise is just that; there are steps, and it takes time to achieve this expertise. Obviously patience is needed to get there. The work and effort is well worth it, but the fact remains, it does take time to get there. What if you could use a simple trick to gain invaluable experience? Would you like to be able to learn to see the markets as an expert over the course of only a few hours? That is what this trick will give you, this is another means of gaining expertise. This is a true favorite of mine, a way for you to "see" the markets for what they are, an ebb and flow of buyers and sellers.

Set aside several hours for this exercise. It is great to do this over four hours, but you can do it with less time if you wish. The length of the exercise is determined by the timeframe of the charts. So if you are looking at the 30-minute charts this will take 30 minutes, if you're looking at four-hour charts this will take four hours. The four-hour charts are my favorite charts, so I love to do this exercise over four hours.

Open a chart, and wait for a new candlestick to appear. If you are watching a shorter timeframe chart, such as the 30-minute chart, after a few minutes, about three minutes or so, take a screenshot of the candlestick. The idea is that you are taking snapshots of the candlestick as it is coming to life. While you are doing this, you should consider what you think is going to happen. It does not matter if you are correct or not, it only matters that you make a guess.

You should take at least six snapshots of your candlestick at equal time intervals. If you are watching a 30-minute candlestick, you should take six snapshots at five-minute intervals. If, however, you are watching a four-hour candlestick, you should take a snapshot at 40-minute intervals, and so forth.

After each snapshot, answer the following questions:

- Is the candlestick now trading higher or lower than the opening price?
- Do you think the candlestick will start trading higher or lower between now and the next snapshot?
- Will this candlestick close as an up (bullish) or as a down (bearish) candlestick?

Do this for all of the snapshots. Watching the candlestick print like this is a lot like watching your child grow up. Maybe in some ways you may be able to anticipate the future, but there will be turning points that are critical, and by recording the candlestick at regular intervals you will be able to see how well you can anticipate the market. The point of this exercise is not to show you how unpredictable the markets are, or to encourage you to get in touch with your inner psychic. The point of this exercise is that, by watching the market, you earn valuable experience. Just as working in a forex tester will help you to get trades on your belt, it is also true that watching a candlestick unfold in a live market is invaluable experience.

At the end of the exercise you will have a slow-motion record of the lifespan of a candlestick. Once the candlestick has finished printing, answer these questions.

- How does the second screenshot of the candlestick differ from the last screenshot of the candlestick?
- Did the candlestick start moving up or down?
- Did the candlestick close in that same direction, or did it end up closing in the opposite direction?
- During which trading session (Asian, European, or North American) did you choose to do this exercise?
- Do you think the results may have been different if you had chosen a different trading session?
- Did the candlestick *after* the one you observed close in the same direction as the candlestick you observed?
- Based on the first two screenshots of the candlestick would you have been able to predict what the candlestick ended up looking like?

If you are interested in really accelerating your trading, do this exercise often. It is quite different to the back-testing in that you are watching the market unfold in real time, just as you would during a live trading session. The most important thing you can learn from doing this exercise is the importance of the closing price.

The closing price is actually critical to the expert naked trader. Think about this: If the closing price is not in the right spot, do you get a kangaroo tail? If the closing price is not in the precise spot for a bullish big shadow, do you have a valid buy signal? If the closing price for a bearish big belt is not near the low, but rather near the middle of the candlestick, is it a valid sell signal? The closing price is absolutely critical to the naked trader.

The real secret to this simple trick is that the opening price of the candlestick does not matter as much as the closing price. Where the candlestick prints during the first two or three snapshots is not as important as where the candlestick ends up, where the closing price is. A slight difference in the closing price can drastically change the look of a price pattern, and is, therefore, why this exercise is so critical, why you can watch a candlestick and see that the beginning of the candlestick is not nearly as important as the closing price.

Think about how much you learned since you began reading this book. Now you should be able to look at a chart and immediately know whether you can take a buy trade, a sell trade, or no trade. Now, you know how to become an expert trader. Not only that, but you know what to focus on to become an expert trader. Now, you know how important the closing price is to your naked trading setups. You should be feeling more confident now. You know precisely the steps you need to take to begin following the path to expert trading. In the next chapter, we will explore confidence in yourself, confidence in your system, what to do when you experience confidence problems, and why losing trades should have nothing to do with your confidence.

CHAPTER 15

Gaining Confidence

Inaction breeds doubt and fear. Action breeds confidence and courage. If you want to conquer fear, do not sit home and think about it. Go out and get busy.
—Dale Carnegie

I magine you have the following:

- A trading system you are comfortable trading.
- A trading system with a very high win rate.
- An incredible amount of money to trade your system.
- All the time you need to trade.
- The best computer and a fast internet connection.

Is this all that you need to trade successfully? Will you find consistent profits with only these things? The answer is no. You need much more than this to trade successfully. To find consistent profits you need to have confidence. In fact, confidence is the most important ingredient for trading success. Confidence will help you profit with an average trading system, but without confidence you will be unable to find success, even with a brilliant trading system.

You will find that there are two different types of confidence problems for forex traders: (1) a lack of confidence in the trading system, or (2) a lack of confidence in yourself.

THE ORIGIN OF CONFIDENCE ISSUES

All traders will have losing streaks. Losing streaks may lead to feelings of inadequacy and disparity. However, if the trading system is a valid winning trading system, it has been tested, and is profitable over the long run, there is probably nothing wrong with the system. Most of the time, a losing streak is due to the wrong application of the trading system. In other words, most losing streaks are due to the misapplication of the system (caused by the trader), and not the system itself.

There are several common issues that many traders have, all of which may lead to losing streaks and confidence issues.

Risk-Management Issues

The next chapter will examine risk in detail. For now, it is important only to note that without proper application of risk management rules, a trading drawdown may be exacerbated and, therefore, may be very difficult to handle for many traders. Traders who have issues with risk management will usually multiply their drawdown and find it difficult to make money consistently. Normal, everyday losing streaks are unfortunate and difficult for many traders to endure, but when these drawdowns are accentuated by poor risk management, the results are often disastrous.

Problems with Discipline

Discipline problems are common. Many traders at banks are not brilliant traders (in fact, many retail forex traders are much better traders than bank traders). Bank traders do not have a sixth sense for the markets. These traders do not have access to secret algorithms or indicators. Many traders are consistently profitable because there is a built-in discipline system at the bank.

Bank traders have a risk manager. The risk manager ensures that the bank trader trades with discipline. The bank hires intelligent trainees to become disciplined traders on the forex desk. The risk manager ensures that the bank traders do not risk too much on their trades.

All the bank traders must follow one simple rule: They must not take more risk than they are allowed. Each bank trader knows how much he may risk, every bank trader has a number, and his risk cannot exceed this number. The risk manager on the forex desk oversees the risk associated with each of the trades taken by the traders. If a trader takes on too much risk, the trader is warned once. If a trader makes this mistake again, the trader loses his job. These are the rules. Each bank trader understands this, and the forex trading desk is set up to tightly manage risk.

The interesting thing about this system is that even those traders who are exceptionally profitable—the traders who make millions for the bank—even these traders are shown the door if they take on too much risk. Banks understand trading is a game of risk. All the bank traders must be disciplined traders. Any trader who steps out of line is a severe concern for the bank.

Retail forex traders such as you and I do not have a risk manager. However, it is possible to re-create the bank system. This is how you can do this: become accountable to someone. Find a trading buddy, your partner, a relative, anyone you respect. Offer them your trading statement each week. This is your report card. Report the risk for each trade. Be accountable to this person. If you take on too much risk (win or lose), your risk manager should reprimand you. Perhaps your "risk manager" will change your trading platform password so you are unable to trade for one week if you take on too much risk. You must learn to keep risk manageable if you want to consistently extract profits from forex trading.

Changing Systems

If you have a losing streak, you may become too careful or too reckless with your trading system. This is a common reaction to a drawdown. This often leads to a downward spiral. It is important to keep track of what you are doing. There are many ways to do this, but be most common way is to keep track of your trading. To make sure that you are not changing your trading rules, do one of the following: Take screenshots of your trades before you take the trade (the set up), during the trade, and after the trade is closed.

You may also want to create a trading journal. This journal should include information such as why you decided to take the trade, the system you employed for the trade, your feelings about the trade, the result of the trade, and a rating on how well you applied the rules of your trading system to that particular trade.

Alternatively, you may set up a video journal; there are many software options for this, some of them freely available on the Internet, but a popular one is called Jing, which will allow you to take a quick recording of your trade. A final option would be to look over your trading printouts—in other words, your trading record. This is another place where you may notice what is happening, why you are changing your trading, and what exactly you are doing that is different to your system.

The key to combating this problem is to become aware, more self-aware of what you are doing as a trader. Just as a professional gardener does not mow the lawn the same way every single week, you may not be taking your trades the same way even though you are trading the same system. Taking records of what you are doing is invaluable for self-assessments later, in order to look at exactly how you are executing your trades and what changes you might be making.

Missing Out

Traders may end up with a losing streak simply because they miss out on some trades. This is a particularly difficult problem for those traders who have a low win rate. It is obviously possible to be a successful and profitable trader—in fact to be a professional trader—with a trading system that has a very low win rate. The problem is that if winning trades do not occur that often, it is imperative that *all* trades are taken to make sure the winners are captured.

If you trade a system that has a low win rate, and you miss out on some of the trades, and these trades end up being large winners, it can be disheartening. Obviously, if you trade a system with a very low win rate, you need large winning trades to maintain profits. Missing out on these winners can be psychologically demoralizing; it can be difficult to maintain your confidence in a trading system with a low win rate. There is an easy solution, however.

If you want to make sure that you do not miss out on trades, or miss out on trading information so that you can manage trades, technology may be your answer. Today, there are many technical solutions for the naked trader. Technology today allows traders to be almost anywhere and still manage the trades.

The key is to be prepared. It is possible for the naked trader to simply trade from a phone. With well-equipped phones, naked traders are able to not only to place trades and manage trades, keeping tabs on live market charts, they can also set alerts. If the market goes to a predetermined price level, traders will receive e-mails or alerts on their phones.

On the Internet, there are services that allow you to set price alerts, so that once the market crosses a price level you receive an e-mail. If you receive e-mails on your phone, you should know nearly immediately if the market reaches a predetermined price. For more information about setting alerts about your charts on your phone, see the video on creating automated alerts at www.fxjake.com/book.

CONFIDENCE IN YOU

Your confidence may ebb and flow; this is part of trading. There are some easy tricks you can do to keep a steady stream of confidence in your trading life. You can do three things, and if you practice these consistently they will help to maintain your confidence.

Step One: The Reasons for Your Success

In order to be confident as a trader, you must consistently execute your trading system as it was outlined in your system rules. More importantly, you must know, without a doubt, the reason why you have chosen to execute your trading system. In other words, your beliefs must align with your trading goals.

This is a foreign concept to most traders. Many traders assume that they want to make money, and if they are not making money, the reason is that they have not found the trading system that will allow them to make money consistently. Notice how the emphasis for most traders is on the *system*. The system yields the reward. The system is responsible for profits. Unfortunately this emphasis on the system is incorrect.

The only traders who do not have to concern themselves with the psychology of trading are those traders who use automated trading systems. You are influencing your trading results regardless of whether you acknowledge this fact. Unless you are trading a purely mechanical system—a pure automated trading system, you are influencing each and every one of your trades. (Here is a test to see if your system is a purely automated system. If you can be away from the Internet for a month and your system will still trade and make money for you, then it is a purely automated system.) Your thoughts, your beliefs, and whether you believe you are deserving of profit all influence how you trade your trading system.

Think about and write down your answers to the following:

- How many wealthy people do you spend time with?
- Do you think that you will one day have a lot of money?
- When something goes wrong with money, do you think that this is "just your luck?"
- When you see a wealthy person, what do you think?
- Do you think that wealthy people are good people?
- If you become extremely wealthy, are you worried that your personality may change?

To learn more about your answers to these questions and your attitudes toward making money, go to www.fxjake.com/book.

Aligning your trading goals with your financial personality is important and something that will occur regardless of whether you are consciously aware of this.

Step Two: The Rewards of Routine

The trading system you employ depends on you. You must identify and execute trades. You must apply the risk management rules to each of your trades. You must remain vigilant and ensure that you take all the trades that your system identifies as high probability trades. In order to achieve all this, you must have an established routine. This routine must be written down, and it must include all the important variables for your trading system.

The rules for your trading system must include your trading routine. Define what you will do, and what you will not do regularly. This will be your trading routine. Adherence to your trading routine is the closest thing you have to insurance against sloppy trading. Sloppy trading involves missing trades, trading the wrong lot size, placing the stop loss at the wrong price, or poor execution when entering a trade.

At a minimum, this is what you should have written down for your trading routine rules:

- When will you look for trades?
- How will you calculate your trade size? (There is a risk-free calculation spreadsheet, a great tool for calculating your trade size, at www.fxjake.com/book.)
- How often will you check the charts?
- How will you be alerted to trading opportunities?
- How will you be alerted when you need to manage your trades?

Defining your trading routine is important because, over time, as you begin to consistently capture profits, you will gain confidence in what you do. The simple act of entering your trade into the risk calculation spreadsheet will often bring an anticipation of profits to come. There is great power in routine.

Step Three: The Machine

If you have aligned your personal beliefs with your trading goals, and if you have designed a well-planned trading routine that you can adhere to, you are now ready to put into place fail-safe rules and tools so you may quickly regain your confidence when it wavers.

The fastest way to regain your confidence is to back-test in a forex tester. A losing streak can be put into proper perspective after you have traded the GBP/USD over three years and found consistent profits in a forex tester using the very same system that has you in a drawdown. Back-testing in general is a one-size-fits-all remedy. Not only does back-testing help your confidence during a losing streak, but it also helps you to concentrate on what is important in your trading system. The simple act of taking 50 trades in a forex tester (or your chosen back-testing software) adds another 50 trades under your belt. You will have honed your skills to identify valid trade set-ups and execute valid trades within the confines of your system.

Spreadsheets can also help you. If you can, make some spreadsheets with the data from your back-testing sessions. These data will help put drawdowns into perspective. There is a great template for you at www.fxjake.com/book. Download the spreadsheet there and enter your back-testing data into the spreadsheet. The spreadsheet will calculate for you the statistics of your trading system. Having the statistics in front of you is evidence that your trading system works, and you may need to trot these data out when you are experiencing a losing streak, to remind yourself that what you are doing is successful trading.

In the next chapter you will see how confidence and risk are related. For now, it is important to note that if you are not following your trading system, that is, if your risk management does not fit with the rules of your trading system, you may find it extremely difficult to execute your system properly.

REASONS FOR LOSING STREAKS

There are many reasons that a trade may not make money. These reasons include the following:

- Poor system execution (mistakes, sloppy trade entry, human error, etc.).
- Changing market (trading system no longer works).
- Bad technology (slow computer, poor Internet connection, etc.).
- Dishonest broker (market manipulation, bad data feed, frozen trading platform, etc.).
- Trading system not flexible enough (unusual market activity, news report, etc.).

All these reasons have one thing in common: They are incorrect. These are not reasons for a losing trade; they are excuses. Confident naked traders understand that these excuses will not aid in the collection of profits from the markets. These reasons for failed trading are excuses; each offers a reason for failure. If you find yourself using these reasons for losing trades, please reconsider your thinking. Changing your thinking about what is possible and what is under your control will help improve your confidence.

Losing trades are really due to one thing—bad luck. Luck will come and go, as you know, so the drawdown you are experiencing will be temporary, and as long as you do not change your rules, you will get it back on track soon. Bad luck is the reason why a trade ends up a loser. Bad luck is the reason you never know if a trade will make money or if it will lose money. The possibility of bad luck is the reason why responsible traders place the same amount of risk on every trade.

If you follow your trading system and all your trading rules, you will have the confidence of knowing that only one thing can lead to a losing trade—bad luck. Luck can neither be accounted for nor can you anticipate your luck. Armed with back-testing data and your trading record (from your live account), you may have a very good idea of the chances that your next trade will be an unlucky one.

The probability that any given trade is a losing trade is calculated as follows:

$$1 - \text{Win Rate}$$

If your trading system has a 59 percent win rate, then you have a 41 percent chance that your very next trade will be an unlucky (losing) trade.

$$1 - 0.59 = 0.41$$

Thinking about your next trade in terms of probabilities may help you to re-focus on what is important: following your trading system. Worrying about any one trade or emphasizing reasons why your trade lost money is not important. The big picture is important, the overall probability of a winning trade is important. A specific trade is not that important.

THE BAD MARKET THEORY

Some traders are concerned that very good trading systems will change the market. The theory goes something like this: If a large proportion of traders start using the kangaroo tail on the daily forex charts, eventually the daily forex charts will stop printing reliable kangaroo tails because too many traders are using kangaroo tails to find high-probability trades. Although the story sounds good, it is incorrect.

Even if *all* the retail forex traders (traders like you and me) traded the daily kangaroo tails, we would not affect the market. There are two reasons why this is true. First, every trader views the market differently, so what is a worthwhile kangaroo tail to me may not be a worthwhile kangaroo tail to you. Second, retail forex traders make up such a small proportion of the forex market that even a truly coordinated trade executed by all retail forex traders would not have an effect on the market. The majority of the volume in forex is from the banks and private funds, not the retail traders. The retail traders make up about 1 percent of all the forex trading volume each day.

The great thing for the naked trader is that naked trading systems are based on market psychology. The naked trading systems you have learned in this book are based on the psychology of the market participants. They are likely to hold for as long as humans participate in the markets. Any downturn in performance is likely due to bad luck if you have been following your system rules. This means that the profits will likely return to normal again, after the bad-luck streak is over.

Finally, the possibility remains that your trading system completely falls apart and stops working. The way to test this is to take a recent sample of all the trades for that system and compare the win rate to the historical win rate. If you are concerned about a recent losing streak for your trading system, compare your historical win rate to the win rate of the past 50 trades. If the historical win rate differs greatly from the current win rate, the trading system may be losing its potency.

CHAPTER 16

Managing Risk

Yes, risk taking is inherently failure-prone. Otherwise, it would be called sure-thing-taking.

—Jim McMahon

A s you progress as a trader you will become involved in thinking and probably reading about trading psychology. Trading psychology is a broad term that encompasses the study of traders and their emotional issues about trading. Trading-psychology literature takes its cues from scientific study of psychology, common sense, and the experience of traders and trading gurus. If you are interested in trading psychology, it probably means that you are further along in your trading education.

If you are one of the traders with an interest in trading psychology, you have moved beyond looking for the perfect trading system. You now understand the important role emotions play in trading results. One thing that many traders fail to recognize is the intricate relationship between what you risk and the emotions you experience during trading. In fact, risk and trading psychology are two sides of the same coin.

YOUR RISK PROFILE

Every battle is won before it is ever fought.

—Sun-Tzu

Some would say your lot in life has been decided. The ending balance of your account is already known. If this were the case, would you like to know who knows this number? Why not ask this person now to find out if you should spend so much of your time trading? Who knows what your final balance will be? Who *is* this person who can tell you what the future holds? Who knows how much money you will make (or lose) due to your trading?

You! This person is you!

You are the one who knows whether you will make money or not, even though you may not have *conscious* access to this information. Most traders do not acknowledge this fact: Your beliefs drive your behaviors. This includes your trading behaviors. If you believe you are worthy of trading profits, you will be able to make money. If you do not believe your trading will lead to profits, you will not be able to consistently make money. It doesn't matter if you decide to work in business or in trading. Your beliefs, whether they are accessible to you consciously, will drive your behaviors.

This is exactly why people who win the lottery end up broke a few years later. This is a very common story. Perhaps you heard about these people. Once they win the lottery, things should change for these lucky winners, but, in fact, it just delays the inevitable result. The end result is, of course, no money. (See the featured story "The Man Who Auctions off His Lottery Winnings.")

The Man Who Auctioned off His Lottery Winnings

William Bud Post, III had a difficult life. His mother died when William was eight, and his father abandoned him and later sent him to an orphanage. As an adult, he drifted between meaningless jobs, working as a spray painter, laborer, cook, and truck driver for the circus. He was unable to afford a home and even spent 28 days in jail for writing bad checks. Even his love life was cursed. He was married and divorced six times.

Then, his luck took a turn for the worse. He won the lottery.

One day, in 1988, he had no job and was receiving a paltry monthly disability check. He had only $2.46 in the bank, so he sold a ring to a pawnshop for $40 and asked his landlady (who was also his on-again-off-again girlfriend, Ann Karpik), to buy 40 lottery tickets with the cash. One of the tickets she bought was the winning ticket. He won $16.2 million.

The lottery payments were to be made over 26 years, and totaled $497,953.47 each year. He spent over $300,000 after receiving the first payment. Bud bought a liquor license, a twin-engine plane (he did not have a pilot's license), a restaurant for his brother and sister, and he bought a used-car lot for his other brother. He was $500,000 in debt three months after his first lottery payment.

In quick succession, things got worse for Mr. Post. He used his second annual payment to purchase a mansion for $395,000 in Oil City, Pennsylvania, with the hopes of refurbishing it. But his former landlady, Ann Karpik, sued him, claiming that they agreed to split any winnings, a claim that Bud denied. The court ruled that Bud owed Ann one-third of his winnings. Bud was unable to pay, so the court ordered him to give Ann his 1992 annual payment. He refused, so the judge froze his future payments. Understandably, visitors to his Pennsylvania mansion noticed that the estate was in disarray, showers were missing, the security malfunctioned (and chirped every 60 seconds), the pool was filled with garbage, there was an old car on blocks in the weedy yard, and the windows were covered with plywood.

Mr. Post was quickly falling into debt, so he hatched a plan. He decided to sell the ailing mansion for $65,000 and auction off his 17 remaining lottery payments in the hopes of scratching out of debt. He hoped that this plan would allow him to hold onto some cash.

His plan failed. Within the year, he had bought a couple of large screen televisions, two homes, three cars, a truck, two motorcycles, some computers, a camper, and a $260,000 sailboat he left in Biloxi, Mississippi. (He had hoped to start a charter fishing business with the boat.)

He was tracked down and arrested on that boat for refusing to serve a prison sentence. He was convicted of assault. Apparently, Mr. Post fired a shotgun at a man who tried to collect a car-repair debt back in Pennsylvania.

Post was quoted as saying "Once I'm no longer a lottery winner, people will leave me alone. That's all I want. Just peace of mind." He said, "I was much happier when I was broke." Post got his wish: After serving his sentence for assault, he was back to living on his $450-per-month disability check.

Why You Win (or Lose)

You win (or lose) because of your beliefs. Specifically, of course I am talking about your winning or losing in the financial game. It does not matter if you are an entrepreneur, looking at establishing a new business, or if you are a salesman, looking to cultivate a stream of customers, or, perhaps more likely, if you are a burgeoning trader, looking to establish reliable trading method to pull profits from the market. The same principles apply to all people looking to make money. Your beliefs about money, and how worthy you believe you are of money will determine whether or not you make money trading.

Perhaps you don't agree. Perhaps you believe that you only need a good trading system in order to find a trading success. If that is the case, then why is it that one profitable trading system may be offered to 10 people, and those 10 people will have varying degrees of success? There are some excellent trading systems in this book. However, not everyone reading this book will take these trading systems and go forward and make money. Why is this the case?

If you believe you are worthy of trading profits you will find they come much more easily. If, however, you believe you do not deserve trading profits, you may never find a trading system that works for you. The most critical aspect of your trading system is you.

Your Money Attitudes

Before you do anything else, do this. Get a piece of paper and a pen. Answer these questions quickly and as truthfully as possible. The important thing here is that you do this now. Be honest and be quick; use your gut reaction to answer in every case.

- True or False? Rich people are good people.
- True or False? Money is the root of all evil.
- True or False? Money comes to those who help others.
- Money is a _____.
- Most rich people are more _____ than most poor people.
- Those with money also have _____.
- Poor people are better _____ than rich people.
- If I had more money, I might become more _____.

Your beliefs about money can determine how much money comes your way. If you believe money is good and you are worthy of wealth, money is more likely to come your way. However, perhaps you believe something different; perhaps you believe that rich people are selfish. Maybe you think that most wealthy people found wealth through immoral behaviors. If you think wealthy people are unethical, you are unlikely to *desire* to become wealthy.

Some traders believe wealthy people are nefarious, and thus these traders are unlikely to ever achieve real wealth. Why should they become wealthy if wealthy people are despicable. Other traders think that rich people simply make loads of money because rich people are very motivated to . . . make money. These traders are much more likely to join the wealthy crowd.

Seeing yourself making money is the first step to trading success. If you believe wealthy people are moral and good, you are more likely to become one of these people. Likewise, if you *know* that you will be making money, if you are confident that you have the skills to achieve wealth, you are on your way to becoming wealthy.

TRADING PSYCHOLOGY AND RISK MANAGEMENT

There are very few laws for trading, but this is one of them: Improper risk management leads to emotional trading problems. Win or lose, if you risk too much on a trade, you will endure emotional problems. It is not only with the losing trades that improper risk management rears its head. Improper risk management—risking too much on a trade—leads to emotional issues, even if the trade is successful. If too much risk is placed in a trade and it ends up a winner, overconfidence, irrational exuberance, and sloppy trade execution may be the result. If too much risk is placed in a trade that ends up being a loser, any number of results may occur: trading rules may be ignored, psychological despair may result, and the management of the trade will almost always be exceptionally poor. There is no way around this law of trading.

Emotional Trading

Emotional issues are always related to your confidence in trading, the current trade in play, or your confidence in the trading system. Emotional issues will creep into your trading regardless of whether you like it. You think that you keep your emotions out of your trading, but, for most traders, this is not true. Most traders get extremely upset after a losing streak, or a losing trade, or missing out on a great trade opportunity. Under most circumstances traders have a very difficult time removing emotion from trading decisions.

However, is it important to remove all emotions from your trading? Is it a bad idea to trade unemotionally? After all, if it is impossible to remove emotions from trading, perhaps you should embrace your emotions. The standard opinion about emotional trading today, most gurus tell us, is that emotional trading is destructive. This is not true. The only destructive trading is trading that is not according to your rules. So whether it is emotional trading or logical trading, if you trade in a manner that is not consistent with you rules, you are trading in a destructive matter.

Emotional trading is the result of improper risk management. When the risk becomes too much, rational reaction to the market is impossible. If you have ever had a trade in which you took a large position—too large a position—and the trade went against you, you know what it is like to try and think when your emotions are running wild.

The antidote to this is to apply proper risk management to your trades, use a well-rehearsed set of trading rules, and apply these over and over again in your trading.

Worst-Case Planning

Worst-case planning means planning for the maximum loss on each trade. This way, the maximum loss cannot hurt you. Over time, by planning for the same loss (your maximum loss, where your stop loss is placed), you will become more efficient in executing your trades. This is the magic of consistent risk management. If each trade has the same risk associated with it, over time you will build up valuable experience with this risk level.

If you keep your risk the same, the worst-case scenario for each and every trade is the same. If you walk outside barefoot on a hot day on the asphalt, your feet may burn. However, if you walk outside every day when it's hot, the asphalt slowly becomes bearable. The same principle applies to drug addicts; over time, drug addicts must take more and more of the same drug to get the same high. This principle of tolerance also applies to traders. It's the tendency for trading execution to become more precise over time when the same amount of money is at risk on every trade. By risking the same percentage of your trading account on every trade, you will become used to the amount of money at risk. You will become immune, over time, to the equity swings in your account with each losing trade, or each winning trade. What will happen, over time, is that you will begin to focus on what is important—executing your trades, and you will not concentrate on the money gained or lost on each trade.

TRADING TOLERANCE

Trading tolerance is the tendency for trading execution to become more precise over time when the same amount of money is at risk on every trade.

Encourage Trading Tolerance

This is how you may encourage trading tolerance. First, calculate your worst-case scenario. This should be the dollar loss if your stop loss is hit. Second, add 20 percent to this amount. Third, use this figure when calculating the risk for your trades. You should assume this (percentage) risk for all of your trades. Finally, use this formula to calculate your risk for each trade. Before long, you will become accustomed to risking this amount. Be prepared to lose this amount. Be prepared for these losing trades, and be prepared for a sequence of losing trades.

Before long, the amount of money will not seem significant, and you will begin to focus on *trade execution*. This is where the money is to be made.

RISKY MONEY TRAPS

Why do most traders fail? Why is trading for consistent profits so difficult? Traders are simply people who look to buy something when it is cheap, and look to sell something when it is expensive. Traders get paid to be bargain hunters and agile market participants. However, there are so many people in the markets who find extreme difficulty attempting to extract profits from the markets.

A close look at the reasons that traders fail—the risky money traps—and how to overcome each of these traps will prepare you for entry into the markets. Remember to consider the other market participants. Many of these people are well capitalized, and they have intelligent people behind the construction and execution of their trading strategies. If you find it difficult to overcome your *own* issues, if you fall into one of the risky money traps before you have entered the markets, you are at a significant disadvantage.

Your Account Is Unprotected

The number-one trading skill you need to succeed as a trader is the ability to *protect your trading account*. This is paramount to all other goals, protecting your account means survival. Traders who are unable to make the jump from novice trader to professional trader fail to recognize the importance of *playing defense*. Professional traders are very good at *playing defense*. Watch the "Tale of Three Trades" video at www.fxjake.com/book for a real market example of how this concept may be applied to live trades. If you can get into the habit of playing defense, you can become a successful professional trader. Learn to recognize the importance of playing defence. Without this you have no chance.

Traders who are unable to protect their money have difficulties with beliefs. These traders may believe they are unworthy of large amounts of money. They may also confuse their belief with the facts. Beliefs may become facts, but traders deal with odds when it matters most.

I may believe the USD/CAD is headed down because the market prints a bearish kangaroo tail on the daily chart. I may decide to risk money based on my belief that the USD/CAD will start trading lower soon. However, this does not make my belief fact. I must wait for the market to tell me whether my *belief* is going to become *market fact*.

If the market instead begins to trade higher and higher and higher, I come to a crossroads. Perhaps I decide on one of the following three courses of action: (1) I may decide to dump the trade because my *belief* seems to be incorrect. (2) I may decide to move my stop loss higher, to give the trade a little more breathing room because I *know* the market will eventually fall. (3) I may even decide to walk away from my computer, to let the market decide whether my belief is correct, knowing that either my stop loss or my profit target will be hit. Two of these reactions (1 and 3) are acceptable means of dealing with my belief, based on the current market activity. The other reaction, 2, is detrimental to my trading account. I have decided to rewrite my trading plan (initial stop loss moved, the trade now has more risk than originally planned for), and I have decided that my belief is market fact, *even when the market provides information to the contrary*.

Think about that. The market has told me that a fair price is higher, not lower. I think the market is headed lower. This is my belief based on the daily bearish kangaroo tail. However, the market trades higher. I *ignore* the market information, the market freely provides me with information about the USD/CAD (the fair market price is higher), and I decide to *assume the opposite is fact*. The market goes up and I decide the market is wrong.

Who do you think will win this battle of wits? Will I win or will the market win?

Remember to keep your beliefs in perspective. There are no beliefs worth more than your entire trading account. You work hard for your money, so defend it. Throw away your beliefs when the market tells you they are incorrect. Keep your money instead.

There are many other beliefs that stand in the way of trading success. Perhaps you are familiar with these risky ideas, such as the I-will-make-it-big-once-I-get-a-big-account idea.

You Need More Screen Time

At times it may seem as though you do not have the time to trade. Among the daily commitments of work, family, and hobbies, it can be difficult to find time to trade. Those missed opportunities can be awful. Simply watching the market march on without you can be more difficult to deal with than the standard-issue losing trade.

Maybe more time in front of the computer will mean more profits? Maybe you think that trading shorter-timeframe charts might multiply your trading opportunities and accelerate your equity curve? Perhaps this is true; if you are able to trade the shorter timeframes you may find more opportunities, if you are able to schedule more screen time, more time in front of your charts.

Please beware that "I need more screen time to trade" is not an excuse for avoiding back-testing. All of your systems should be vetted with back-testing results, forward-testing results, and the smaller live-trading account.

Most traders will use this excuse to create a case for leaving a job, and this thinking is a dangerous place to be. Many traders are not quite ready to start trading full-time, but they think that by leaving their full-time permanent jobs, the added screen time will push them over the top and make it easier for them to achieve trading success. Sadly, this is often not true.

Your Job Is Holding You Back

Related to the I-need-more-screen-time trap is the I-gotta-dump-my-job trap. Traders fantasize that more time, specifically more screen time, will help them to achieve consistent profits. A little more focus will bring the results they are looking for in their trading.

This seems logical, but it rarely works. Putting yourself in a situation in which you *need* to make money consistently from your trading account, before you have learned how to consistently make money from your trading, is a bad idea. You would not expect a stuttering game show contestant to be able to rattle off quiz answers with the pressure of the clock ticking down, would you? This is why it makes sense for you to take the proper steps, starting with back testing, moving to forward testing, then on to small account trading, before you ever begin trading for a living, trading your large trading account.

Unrealistic expectations may also affect your trading. It may be tempting to backward engineer your trading profits. Perhaps you decide to trade the daily charts, and you would like to make $15,000 per month from your trading. You decide that you need to make 500 pips each month and trade for $30 per pip. $30 per pip × 500 pips = $15,000; simple math provides you with your trading goal.

What if your trading account contains only $35,000? You may have to be very careful. If you are trading at $30 per pip and your stop loss is 100 pips away from your entry price (certainly possible with a daily chart trade), you are risking $3,000 on your trade, that is 8.5 percent of your trading account at risk. Three losing trades such as this one and you would be down over 30 percent on your trading account. This is why many traders have a difficult time making the jump from part-time to full-time trader, your *nice-to-have*-profits turn into *must-have* profits; the focus is on the money and not the trading results.

Thinking about trading in terms of *money* is precisely why many part-time traders want to leave their full-time jobs. It is also the reason many part-time traders find consistently profitable trading so elusive once they leave their jobs. Remember to concentrate on your trading, execute each trade as best you can. The money will come if you concentrate on becoming a *better trader*.

You Need a Bigger Account

Some traders insist on holding to the idea that only larger trading accounts will allow for success. The idea is that the giant trading account in the sky will bring some sort of nirvana. Unfortunately, for many of the reasons listed earlier in this chapter (namely, attitudes toward money and wealthy people), the opposite is actually true.

The great majority of traders around the world do much better trading when placing trades in very small accounts. Once traders move up to larger accounts, in most circumstances these traders end up thinking too much about the money and too little about managing trades according to their system rules.

It is possible to do exceptionally well, even if you start off with a very small trading account. The focus should be on trading your system. Your effort should be placed on executing and managing your trades as closely as possible to the rules of your system. If you move away from trading your system and instead focus on the dollar amounts, you will likely see your performance suffer. If you have issues with money and wealthy people, you are *sure* to see your performance suffer.

The idea that a large trading account will help you achieve your financial goals may be comforting, but until you have been able to successfully manage your smaller trading account, and until you deal with your beliefs about wealthy people and money, trading a large trading account will probably be little more than frustrating.

Large is, of course, a relative word. For some traders a large account would be an account of $10,000, and for other traders an account size of $150,000 is small. Think about this: the idea that a few traders may see an account and think that it is very small and other traders may see the same account and think that it is a very large account. The fact that traders can view the same account very differently is more evidence for the idea that traders' attitudes and beliefs toward money will drastically effect how well traders make money and sound trading decisions.

So if you find yourself thinking, "I need a bigger trading account so I will really be able to make some serious money," make sure that you are making serious money with your smaller accounts first. A larger account may simply make trading more difficult if you are not prepared for the challenge.

Thinking That Trading Is Easy

Maybe you think that consistently profitable trading is easy. Perhaps you have scrolled back on some charts and identified the wonderful opportunities staring back at you. These opportunities may come in the form of kangaroo tails and big shadows at market turning points, those places where the market offers a clue about what will happen next. You may become confident that successful trading can be yours. Maybe you begin to think that profitable trading can be *easy*.

Be careful of this overconfidence that often appears as the successful-trading-is-easy idea. Trading successfully can be *simple*, but that does not make it easy. Trading successfully will mean putting in the time back testing your system, developing a trading plan to cover all of the what-if scenarios you can come up with, and creating a method for overcoming the doldrums of the inevitable drawdowns. Planning is critical for you to succeed in the long term, but it is not the only ingredient for success.

To succeed you will need a healthy dose of determination. History is littered with stories of famous people who overcame adversity, people who accepted success because failure was not an option. Determination is the common thread among these stories. Walt Disney took three years (double the anticipated 18 months) to produce a movie that went over budget by 400 percent. All the while, people surrounding him questioned whether his full-length cartoon movie would have any mass appeal. The movie was an overwhelming success—you may have heard of *Snow White*. Another man had an altogether different life experience. His mother died when he was nine. His friend lent him money to run a business, and a year later he lost the business and went bankrupt. He ran for public office on *five* occasions and lost each time. The love of his life died before he could marry her. He suffered a nervous breakdown. His second son died at a young age. You may know him as Abraham Lincoln, the sixteenth president of the United States. Another famous person began life as a child in a poor household. She was the result of a one-night stand. Her mother worked as a maid. Her father was in the military when she was born. As a young child, she lived with her grandmother in poverty, often wearing dresses made of potato sacks. She was sexually abused by her cousin, her uncle, and a family friend from the age of nine. She ran away from home, became pregnant, and her child died soon after his birth. Despite this dubious start in life, Oprah Winfrey became a millionaire at age 32 and is considered the richest woman in entertainment. She has acted in movies, co-authored five books, and inspires millions who watch her television shows and read her magazines.

Each of these people share one thing in common: determination. You simply must have determination to succeed in trading (or any other endeavor). All successful people share determination. Your determination will guide you to trading expertise in the form of all the hours spent in front of charts, back-testing. Your determination will yield resourcefulness when it is needed most, during drawdowns and when your confidence is shaken. Your determination will help aid you to see your success before it appears. Determination is your ride to success. Let it carry you to where you want to be.

You know what to do now. The question remains: Are you determined to succeed as a naked trader?

About the Trading Software and Video Tutorial

I n order to improve your trading, a special members' area is available on the web to supplement the concepts laid out in this book. At this special link you'll find interactive tutorials and a FREE software tool, including:

- **Support and Resistance Interactive Video Tutorial:** Gain confidence when trading with Support/Resistance by implementing my proprietary rules as laid out in this tutorial.
- **Big Shadow Interactive Tutorial:** Master the step-by-step rules to trading my favorite and simplest yet most successful strategy by watching this interactive tutorial.
- **Support and Resistance Software:** Trade side by side with me, using this cutting-edge software that sends my S&R lines right to your trading charts, in real time.

Go to www.fxjake.com/book to create an account and access the FREE Naked Trading members' area today!

About the Authors

Alex Nekritin

Alex Nekritin has been a professional trader for more than 10 years and is the founder and president of TradersChoiceFX.com. TradersChoiceFX is a forex-introducing brokerage firm that is able to enhance its clients' forex trading success by matching them up with the best fit forex dealer for them.

Alex's specialties include risk management and system development. He has a degree with a concentration in investment banking and derivative instruments from Babson College in Massachusetts.

Walter Peters, PhD

Before becoming a professional trader, Walter Peters worked as a clown, magician, online market researcher, and jury consultant. Dr. Peters has a PhD in experimental psychology and an extensive background in statistics.

As a naked forex trader, Dr. Peters enjoys trading simple trading systems. He has a keen interest in trading psychology and how trading beliefs yield trading results. He trades with forex traders around the world on his website www.fxjake.com a place for naked traders. When he is not trading, Dr. Peters enjoys spending time in the ocean and talking about trading.

Index